ELIZABETH JACKSON

THE

Faith

AND

Fire

within

us

AN AMERICAN CREDO

THE UNIVERSIT̶ OTA PRESS

Copyright 1944 by the

UNIVERSITY OF MINNESOTA

Ga. 1⁸⁰(2⁰⁰)

PRINTED AND BOUND BY

W. B. CONKEY COMPANY

HAMMOND, INDIANA

Foreword

THIS is a book about ideas. It is not an anthology, although it is full of quotations, and it is in no sense literary history or literary criticism. It is not wholly what its subtitle promises, an American credo; it claims to be nothing more than a conviction about other people's convictions: "I believe that *we* believe . . ." The separate chapters are essays in the literal sense of the word, *attempts*—attempts to discover, describe, and estimate the beliefs that underlie American society.

One consequence of the present war has been to stimulate this kind of inquiry. No one person can examine more than a fraction of the evidence, and no two people, perhaps, will interpret their findings in exactly the same way, but no matter how much we disagree we shall certainly be better off for having scrutinized the patterns of our thinking. We are a believing people, and we do well to pause from time to time and consider the substance of our creed.

Some readers will be surprised that in a discussion of ideas I give so much space to poetry. There is a popular fallacy that poetry is silly stuff, all about love and roses. There is also a theory, cherished by many true lovers of books, that the intellectual element in poetry is something to be ignored. "Poetry is not the thing said but a way of saying it." "Meaning is of the intellect, poetry is not." Such ideas, I believe, are contradicted by the direct testimony of the poets themselves and by their poetry. The preponderance of the evidence is all the other way. Generally speaking, poets have written poetry because they have had important things to say and wanted to say them as well as possible.

They have talked, and they have made people listen to them. For words are things, as Byron said, and the words of poetry have an astonishing efficacy.

> But words are things, and a small drop of ink,
>   Falling like dew, upon a thought, produces
> That which makes thousands, perhaps millions, think.

"I knew a very wise man," wrote Fletcher of Saltoun, "that believed that if a man were permitted to make all the ballads, he need not care who should make the laws of a nation." "Poets," said Shelley, "are the unacknowledged legislators of the world."

> One man with a dream, at pleasure,
>   Shall go forth and conquer a crown;
> And three with a new song's measure
>   Can trample an empire down.

These are all exaggerations, but exaggerations of an incontestable truth. When poetry adds excitement to philosophy it becomes one of the most potent forces yet discovered. I doubt if anyone could give a just estimate of the mind of a nation without knowing what poetry it had written and what poetry it had read.

As a matter of fact, the longer I live with books, the less I find myself inclined to dwell upon distinctions between poetry and prose or to draw hard and fast lines between first-rate literature and second-rate, or even between literature and journalism. There are great books, to be sure, that stand out above all the rest, but these are not the only ones that we live by. In choosing quotations for this book I have thought primarily of ideas and have put poetry and prose, epic and radio talk side by side. Here are a few hundred quotations (out of what might have been many thousands) all bearing in some way or other on the interpretation of modern America. They will suggest, among other things, I hope, the variety and complexity of our intellectual ances-

iv

try, the continuity of English and American thinking, the constant interrelation of literature and life, and the importance in our civilization of that liberty which Milton put above all others, "the liberty to know, to utter, and to argue freely according to conscience."

I cannot conclude this foreword without expressing my indebtedness to Margaret S. Harding of the University of Minnesota Press, for seeing that there was a place for such a book, for insisting on having it written, and for giving me the benefit of her wisdom and experience in the writing.

E. J.

Contents

I   Such People as We Are

Now that the seas are limed
With fire, and a fathom under
Water spouts prepare,
In the salt cold, their thunder;

Now that the land is warm
For the due rain, for the seed,
But war birds, dropping sulphur
Drone, and the borders bleed;

Now that the ways are strangled,
Now that the best has been,
Where lies the hidden pathway
Verity walked in?

MARK VAN DOREN, *Crisis*

The importance of the history of a country depends, not upon the splendour of its exploits, but upon the degree to which its actions are due to causes springing out of itself.

HENRY THOMAS BUCKLE, *History of Civilization in England*

By the soul
Only, the Nations shall be great and free.

WILLIAM WORDSWORTH, *Near Dover, September 1802*

The sensual and the dark rebel in vain,
Slaves by their own compulsion!

SAMUEL TAYLOR COLERIDGE, *France: an Ode*

It is a strange thing—to be an American.

. . . .

Neither a place it is nor a blood name.
America is West and the wind blowing.
America is a great word and the snow,
A way, a white bird, the rain falling,
A shining thing in the mind and the gulls' call.
America is neither a land nor a people,
A word's shape it is, a wind's sweep—

ARCHIBALD MACLEISH, *American Letter*

The main shapes arise!
Shapes of Democracy total, result of centuries,
Shapes ever projecting other shapes,
Shapes of turbulent manly cities,
Shapes of the friends and home-givers of the whole earth,
Shapes bracing the earth and braced with the whole earth.

WALT WHITMAN, *Song of the Broad-Axe*

IF YOU want information about American ideas and ideals, now is the time to get it. Almost anyone will be more than willing to instruct you. The radio, the movies, periodicals, and newspapers all repeat the same message. For people who like to buy their ideas neatly and compactly bound, there is a steady stream of anthologies pouring from the press. Nearly every day I get publishers' announcements of new variants on the themes of Voices of Freedom and Democratic Traditions. It is universally agreed that we Americans believe in a large number of noble ideals and have been believing in them ever since 1775 or 1620 or the Magna Charta or possibly since the days of the prophet Isaiah—freedom, democracy, equality, the sacredness of the

2

individual, justice, tolerance, free speech, universal education, good fellowship, courage, righteousness, and peace.
All the editors, all the writers and speakers agree that these
are the things we believe in. Certainly it is a splendid list.
The books are impressive and, what is more, full of good,
straight statements that ought to be reprinted oftener between wars.

No wonder we are the greatest nation in the world! No
wonder the peoples of the earth flocked to our gates in the
years when, as Lowell put it, we had room about our hearth
for all mankind! With such ideals everywhere among us,
who can set a limit to the glories of the years to come?

Then I pick up my evening paper. Somehow or other
there seems to be a sudden change in the atmosphere. There
are black markets in one city and race riots in another. In
one city after another the disagreements between employer
and employees have reached a deadlock. A school commit-
tee has refused an offer of free lunches for undernourished
children on the ground that this might start them on the
road to communism. A manufacturer is indicted for chisel-
ing on war contracts and explains that he chiseled only a
reasonable amount. An exceptionally fine soldier is refused
a commission in the army because he once fought for democracy in Spain. Another man is struck off the government payroll because he has been denouncing fascism ever
since the march on Rome instead of merely since Pearl
Harbor. A congressman is horrified to discover that in-
terned Nisei are permitted a certain small measure of self-
government. A southern statesman proposes a plank of
"white supremacy" in the next Democratic platform. Not
to mention kidnapping, rape, and murder as usual. Are these
the concrete evidences of our faith in democracy, justice,
tolerance, and good fellowship?

In fact, if you wanted to prove the complete fatuity of
American professions of faith and draw up an indictment

3

of American democracy in general, could you do better than to go through the last year's file of *PM* or the *New York Times* or your own home-town newspaper? In the years before the war I used to read German descriptions of manners and customs in America. I remember one sketch of American domestic life in which the men sat with their feet on the mantelpiece, ate raw beefsteak two inches thick, and spat their chewing gum against the wall. Yet I can't remember any fantasy more absurd than last year's record —if you look only at certain things. If half the items in the papers are true, how in the world do we expect to win a war? Why *should* we win a war? What in the world would we do with the victory after we won it?

These are rhetorical questions. They need not be answered. It would be easier to write poetry about them.

> Things fall apart; the centre cannot hold;
> Mere anarchy is loosed upon the world,
> The blood-dimmed tide is loosed, and everywhere
> The ceremony of innocence is drowned;
> The best lack all conviction, while the worst
> Are full of passionate intensity.

If Yeats wrote those lines twenty years ago, what would he write now?

And yet, oddly enough, we do seem to be winning the war. A large number of our boats, guns, and men get to the right places at the right times, and they do a very satisfactory amount of damage. American army officers are pulling off one good job after another, and American soldiers are going to town. We appear to be nobler in the Solomons and the Mediterranean than in Washington or New York or any of their sister cities, just as we are much, much nobler in the anthologies than in the newspapers. Are the noble sentiments all fakes, or are the newspapers all liars? Are all the best Americans either dead or in the Army? Or does the Army work such a miraculous transformation in American human nature that we ought to pray to be at war all the time? These also are rhetorical questions.

This is an odd beginning for a book which is essentially a profession of faith in America and American ideas. I admit freely that we are capable of all the acts of folly, selfishness, and wickedness recorded in the daily press, but I am still ready to argue that fundamentally we are a right-thinking, right-acting nation with a sound faith in all the virtues on Page One. Oh, you say, so now you are going to prove that we are a well-meaning people? What could be more damning?

On the other hand, suppose we were ill-meaning? Suppose we established special schools to train boys in race-rioting and lynching? Suppose we proclaimed as our creed an undying faith in slavery, injustice, intolerance, suspicion, and war?

Just let me give an illustration. Here is a story from William Shirer's *Berlin Diary*. As everyone knows, Germany imposes heavy penalties for listening to foreign broadcasts. A certain woman had been officially notified that her son in the *Luftwaffe* was missing and must be presumed dead. Eight of her neighbors, listening surreptitiously to a forbidden London broadcast, heard his name read out in a list of English prisoners. They wrote individually to reassure her. Whereupon everyone who sent her the news found himself arrested for having listened to a foreign radio station. When Shirer tried to tell the story on the radio, "the Nazi censor cut it out on the ground that American listeners would not understand the heroism of the woman in denouncing her eight friends!"

Of course we don't know anything about that woman. She may have been a horrid woman to start with. Maybe she had always hated her neighbors. Maybe she hated her son. In any case, she was outnumbered by the kindhearted neighbors. But can you imagine that happening in America?

5

Can you imagine a whole American city controlled by a system of subsidized tale-bearing? Or any American national agency that would rejoice in this kind of patriotism? Take a poll of public opinion anywhere in America and ask, "Which do you approve of, the woman or the neighbors?" Have you any doubt how the vote would stand?

Let me tell another story, this time a news item that came from the Spanish Civil War. One of Franco's men, a peasant, had been wounded and taken prisoner and knew that he was dying. He asked for a priest, but there was no priest to be had. He tried to say the Pater Noster, but he had not said it since childhood and the words would not come. A Loyalist soldier, himself an atheist, sat down by the dying Catholic and said the Pater Noster for him. He said it very slowly and carefully, one phrase at a time, so that the man could repeat it after him. Then he made a cross of two sticks tied together, put it into the man's hands, stayed with him until he died, buried him, and set up the cross upon the grave.

I don't know the nationality of the Loyalist soldier. Probably he was Spanish. He might have been American or English. Whatever his nationality, he believed in kindness and freedom of thought. Although the cross was to him the symbol of a church that he hated and the Pater Noster a piece of pernicious priestly jargon, he could deal reverently with both cross and prayer in order to give a half hour's comfort to a dying enemy.

Tell that story anywhere in America and ask, "Do you approve of that Loyalist soldier? Do you think that was an American way to behave?" I cannot believe there would be much doubt about the answer to either question.

Let me make a more fantastic supposition. Imagine a sort of supernatural and transcendental Gallup poll that was not merely a sampling but a complete and accurate record of American opinions. Suppose we could find out what Americans actually think about equality, justice, tolerance, free speech, and all the things on our first list, along with a few others like kindness, honesty, and courage. I think that we would stack up about as well as any country available for comparison. Certainly we would show a splendid percentage of people who are sure of their convictions about these things. There isn't a corner grocery in the country where you can't start an argument about convictions. You would have to hunt a long, long time for a man who said, "I think what the Fuehrer thinks; the Fuehrer is always right." Moreover, the total body of beliefs would be pretty admirable and pretty idealistic. And in the third place, though this is the hardest thing to prove, I believe there would be an astonishingly large number of people whose conduct conforms substantially to their professions of faith.

Notice that I have put this comparatively. *As people go,* in comparison with a couple of dozen other nations who may or may not be our allies, we show up very well. I was astonished recently to find an even more explicit statement in an article by President Hutchins of the University of Chicago. "Though we can hardly be said to practice freedom, law, equality, justice, and democracy," says President Hutchins, "we are *further along that road than any other nation.*"

I have italicized the final words because, coming from a man who is notoriously critical of American civilization, they seem to have the force of italics. He goes on to say that at the very least words like freedom and democracy are the ones on which we have been brought up. "No political leader has yet dared to call upon Americans to espouse the cause of inequality, injustice, and tyranny." He might have added that anything that calls for public approval has to be advertised as just and democratic. Even child labor and the poll tax have been defended as essential to democracy—which goes to show, I suppose, that our intelligent

7

comprehension of democracy lags far behind our faith in the general idea.

We are, after all, fairly ordinary specimens of the genus homo. We are stupid and we are selfish. Selfishness and stupidity are as much a part of us as hands and feet. They work like the inertia and friction that we studied in elementary physics. A stationary body tends to remain stationary; inherited evils tend to stay as they are. A moving body is accompanied by predictable forces that slow it down; any human attempts at reform or improvement will be subject to the same kind of drag. We should take these things into account as we judge ourselves, always remembering that there is a difference between recognizing selfishness as a law of nature and exalting it into a major virtue.

We must realize also that there exist, even in people like us, vast potentialities for active and destructive evil. Some years ago, before Hitler and his party came into power, George Edgar Vincent was warning us of the difficulties in the way of lasting peace among nations. There were obstacles, he said, that the idealists always left out of account—"deep-seated, emotional aversion to strangers, biologically entrenched racial prejudice, the pleasures of hate."

The pleasures of hate; the pleasures of cruelty. These are things that civilized life keeps in abeyance. There are chapters about them in the books on abnormal psychology, and college sophomores study them and memorize the technical terms that identify them. In peacetime we read of isolated outbursts of beastliness and shudder at them and then forget the horror as though these things were entirely foreign to our constitution. We do wrong. Stevenson talks about respectable married people, with umbrellas, living on the sides of volcanoes. There are volcanoes in human nature, and none of them are ever extinct; we all of us live on their slopes. In the old peaceful days we used to read horrible stories of martyrdoms and inquisitions and St. Bartholo-

8

mew's Day massacres, and say, "This is all ancient history. It could never happen in our world." Again we were wrong. We have seen cruelty today bursting forth in volcanic eruption. More than that, we have seen it glorified as a splendid flame-flower of patriotism. It is against such a background as this that we must set up our study of American ideals.

It is our great good fortune to have inherited a civilization that for centuries has imposed restraints upon the lawless impulses of man. It is not that we have changed human nature. Pride, gluttony, covetousness, lust, envy, anger, and sloth are still part of the human mechanism as surely as when the medieval theologians first set them down as the Seven Deadly Sins, but in the course of centuries they have been curbed by custom and education. Anger has been made to keep its place; the angry child is taught to count ten. Gluttony, once respectable and even aristocratic, is now regarded with contempt. Sloth is so much in disrepute that a restless busyness is one of our commonest attributes. Covetousness and envy find themselves counteracted by ideals of generosity and fair play.

One of the natural fruits of anger is intolerance. Tolerance is not a virtue that comes to any of us naturally; it has to be cultivated. It requires not only faith in its desirability but self-control and long practice. It has been a favorite subject of conversation in England and America for more than two hundred years, and yet it is still far from reaching perfection among us. Benjamin Franklin always made a point of defending Locke on *Toleration* and Jeremy Taylor on *The Liberty of Prophesying*. When anyone argued that intolerance was commanded by the Scriptures, Franklin would call for a Bible, open it solemnly at the fifty-first chapter of Genesis, and read aloud.

And Abraham was standing at the door of his tent looking by the way of the wilderness and behold a man came leaning on his staff, and Abraham said unto the man, Stranger, turn in,

9

and tarry with me this night, and the man answered and said unto Abraham, Nay! but I will tarry under this oak. And Abraham pressed him and he turned in.

And Abraham set meat before him, but the man called not on the Lord to bless it; wherefore Abraham was wroth; and turned him out by the way whence he came.

Now at midnight the Lord called unto Abraham and Abraham said, Here am I, Lord—and the Lord said unto him, Where is the stranger? Abraham answered and said unto the Lord: He would not call on thy name to bless his meat; wherefore I turned him out with blows.

And the Lord said unto Abraham, Have I not borne with him this hundred and sixty and eight years, and couldest not thou, who are thyself a sinner, bear with him one night?

Franklin died more than a hundred and fifty years ago, and we have still not learned the lesson of that apocryphal chapter of Genesis. Yet, as President Hutchins might say, we are further along the road than almost any other nation. In spite of all the evidence to the contrary there are substantial proofs that tolerance is part of our habit of thought. It is characteristically American that the Harvard Memorial Chapel commemorates not only the three hundred and seventy-three men who died for the cause of the Allies in the First World War but also the three Harvard men who died in the German service. I know churches today where the names of conscientious objectors stand on the same honor roll with the names of the men in the armed forces. To many of us it seems reasonable that they should, but fathers of boys in the South Pacific grit their teeth as they pass by. "Those boys on the same list with *my* boy!" But the fathers and mothers *do* pass by without demonstration. They don't spit on the names or tear the record from the wall or boycott the minister; the lists still stand as a testimony to our American faith in the virtue of tolerance.

On the whole, as Americans we are inclined to be pleased with ourselves. Our armies are the best armies, and our virtues are the best virtues. Do we realize, I wonder, how much

depends on our ability to maintain not only those armies but
those virtues?

> In the nightmare of the dark
> All the dogs of Europe bark,
> And the living nations wait,
> Each sequestered in its hate.

So wrote Auden in 1939. A younger poet, Nicholas Moore,
saw the nightmare coming closer.

> I am the man of Paris and Madrid,
> The man with a cloud of disaster over my head,
> And faster, in England here, it comes on me, the wind
> That blows only this nightmare on mankind,
> That shows the fascist strong, and the democrat blind . . .

Will the mad dogs of human nature break loose among
ourselves? Will the nightmare overwhelm even the free nations? Or have we the strength to hold fast the civilization
it has taken us so many centuries to develop? Can we keep
ourselves true to the faith that has come down to us? William Vaughn Moody was asking himself such questions as
these when he wrote "An Ode in Time of Hesitation,"
standing, as he said, "before the solemn bronze Saint Gau-
dens made . . . to the good memory of Robert Shaw." He
let his mind dwell on the great heritage of American faith,
and then he listened to the noisy and discordant voices
around him. Was America still a country in which men died
for an ideal, or was she selling herself to hate and greed?

> Are we the eagle nation Milton saw
> Mewing its mighty youth,
> Soon to possess the mountain winds of truth,
> And be a swift familiar of the sun
> Where aye before God's face his trumpets run?
> Or have we but the talons and the maw,
> And for the abject likeness of our heart
> Shall some less lordly bird be set apart? —
> Some gross-billed wader where the swamps are fat?
> Some gorger in the sun? Some prowler with the bat?

Ah no!
We have not fallen so.
We are our fathers' sons: let those who lead us know!

Today the confusion of voices is even more bewildering. Different tongues tell different tales, and I can make no pretense of untangling all the contradictions. Yet even in the midst of chaos I can find the same assurance that gave comfort to Moody. "We are our fathers' sons." We have inherited our fathers' faith. As President Hutchins says, we were brought up on the right words. The great books are still on our shelves and easy to open. It ought to be worth while to spend an hour or two finding out what they have to tell us.

One more point. I started with our faith in democracy, but that is not the thing about which I shall find the most to say. We believe in democracy, well and good; but even more important is the fact that we believe in the things that make democracy possible. We believe in kindness, tolerance, honesty, intelligence, and courage. If we can make democracy work, it is not simply because the system is good, or even because we believe in it. Rather it is because we are the sort of people who can live together that way. We have the right qualities for life in a democratic state. Let us look for a short while at those qualities and the ways in which they came to be ours.

II The English-Speaking Peoples

Great men have been among us;
        hands that penned
And tongues that uttered wisdom—better none:
The later Sidney, Marvel, Harrington,
Young Vane, and others who called Milton friend.

WILLIAM WORDSWORTH, *Great Men Have Been among Us*

Gentleness, Virtue, Wisdom, and Endurance—
These are the seals of that most firm assurance
    Which bars the pit over Destruction's strength.

PERCY BYSSHE SHELLEY, *Prometheus Unbound*

To Mercy, Pity, Peace, and Love
All pray in their distress;
And to these virtues of delight
Return their thankfulness.

WILLIAM BLAKE, *The Divine Image*

Blow bugles, blow! They brought us, for our dearth,
    Holiness, lacked so long, and Love, and Pain.
Honour has come back, as a king, to earth,
    And paid his subjects with a royal wage;
And Nobleness walks in our ways again;
    And we have come into our heritage.

RUPERT BROOKE, *The Dead*

An American Credo

I think continually of those who were truly great.
Who, from the womb, remembered the soul's history
Through corridors of light where the hours are suns
Endless and singing.
. . . .
Near the snow, near the sun, in the highest fields
See how these names are fêted by the waving grass
And by the streamers of white cloud
And whispers of wind in the listening sky.
The names of those who in their lives fought for life
Who wore at their hearts the fire's center.
Born of the sun they travelled a short while towards the sun,
And left the vivid air signed with their honour.

STEPHEN SPENDER, *I Think Continually of Those*

I HAVE often wished there was some single word in our language that meant "characteristic of the inhabitants of the British Isles, the United States, Canada, Australia, New Zealand, and the Union of South Africa, together with their ancestors, relatives, and descendants." I have thought of this particularly in these years when we have been fighting the same war and reiterating the professions of a common faith. The need comes to me with new force whenever I read a paragraph like the one that a London editor wrote about Leslie Howard immediately after his death.

Leslie Howard . . . achieved his entirely deserved success by the art with which he externalised his own qualities—gentleness, humour, vagueness, unostentatious courage, sensibility and a genuine and unusual modesty. These are qualities that make up an ideal English type which no one could present more pleasingly. (I am told that he was half Hungarian!) . . . His friends mourn one of the most charmingly affectionate of men, the public has lost an excellent artist and an irreplaceable champion of Anglo-American understanding.

The parenthetical "half Hungarian" is in recognition of the fact that the English lay no claim to "race" in the Nazi sense. The true-born Englishman, as Defoe pointed out in 1701, is a mongrel.

> A true-born Englishman's a contradiction,
> In speech an irony, in fact a fiction.

This "mongrel half-bred race," as Defoe described it, has left its own small island and crossed oceans and established its civilization in the vast territories of the New World and the South Seas, growing ever more miscellaneous in blood and breed and yet still giving birth to minds and manners such as Shakespeare knew. It can produce men like Leslie Howard, whose qualities of spirit delighted movie-goers all round the English-speaking world. (I have read that Goering detested him.) He made a splendid hero for anti-Nazi movies because the things he stood for in the stories were the things that the English-speaking peoples think they stand for themselves. He may have been, as the editor put it, an ideal English type, but he was a type by no means confined to one small island.

As I say, we need an adjective that we haven't got. The word *English* itself we use sometimes loosely and sometimes very narrowly. If we speak of the English climate we mean specifically the weather of the southern half of the island of Great Britain. By English literature, on the other hand, we may mean either books written in England or books written in English, and by the English language we mean that language—wherever, whenever, however, and by whomsoever spoken. It would help our Anglo-American understanding, to repeat the phrase, if the word could be applied to people and ideas in the same all-inclusive way. We could say that it is English (and also American) to believe in constitutional government, and British (but not American) to combine constitutional government with hereditary monarchy. Leslie

15

Howard's qualities were English in the sense that they were also American.

There is a building at the foot of Kingsway in London with a dedication carved on the architrave in large capitals: TO THE FRIENDSHIP OF THE ENGLISH-SPEAKING PEOPLES. I have never gone past that building without reading the words, and I have never read them without being glad that they were there. The adjective "English-speaking" is certainly good in its way, in that it suggests that the bond between us is not race but language and therefore, by implication, things said and things thought. On the other hand, the word is cumbersome and unhandy in a sentence. You can't say, "It is very English-speaking to like games and sports" or even "It is very English-speaking to make puns."

Apart from the grammatical difficulty, "the English-reading peoples" or "the English-thinking peoples" would get closer to the heart of the matter. Spoken English implies a pronunciation, and differences in accent are among the most irritating things in the world. Not Galsworthy or Hugh Walpole or even Edgar Wallace could have won international popularity by reading his own books out loud. I once met an Englishman on leave from an army post in India. He found that Americans were always appealing to him for footnotes to Kipling. It was extraord'n'ry, he said, perfectly extraord'n'ry. "*I* didn't know that Americans read Kipling. And I don't see how you can when you can't *pronounce* him!" Yet we all knew the same poems that he did and recited them in chorus, and we often felt that it was *his* accent that failed to do Kipling justice!

It is the written word far more than the spoken word, I believe, that binds the English-speaking peoples together. I am not thinking of the eight hundred words of Basic English, though doubtless they have their uses, but of the hundred thousand or more that we have been combining and recombining for centuries in an infinitely complex fab-

ric of association. It is by virtue of this that Winston
Churchill can stir the same kinds of emotion in men ten
thousand miles apart.

We shall fight in France, we shall fight on the seas and oceans,
we shall fight with growing confidence and growing strength
in the air. . . . We shall fight on the beaches, we shall fight on
the landing grounds, we shall fight in the fields and in the
streets, we shall fight in the hills; we shall never surrender.

The "landing grounds" belong to the twentieth century
only, but all the other words—"the seas and oceans," "the
beaches," "the hills"—are loaded with association. "We shall
fight . . ." "I have fought a good fight, I have finished my
course, I have kept the faith." "Fight the good fight with
all thy might." "From the halls of Montezuma, To the
shores of Tripoli, We fight our country's battles in the air,
on land and sea."

>   Well hast thou fought
> The better fight, who single hast maintained
> Against revolted multitudes the cause
> Of truth.

The lines come into your mind faster than you can write
them down. The English (English-thinking?) tradition is
full of fighting sentences, and Mr. Churchill has not been
a parliamentary orator for forty years without knowing
how to remind us of the right things. There is a pretty uniform conviction in the English-speaking world that people
who are ready to fight to the last ditch are the right sort
of people.

It has always interested me to see how the English idea
of character has developed through the centuries and yet
not changed in any essential way since the days of Chaucer.
Concepts have crossed the Atlantic and been modified by
the forces of the younger nations and then gone back to
give new strength and courage to English ideas at home.
I am thinking not so much of theory, flat and expository,

as theory brought to life in poetry and story. One of the best places to look for this kind of thing is in *The Faerie Queene*.

I think there is cause for regret that *The Faerie Queene* is rarely read today except in formal courses in literature. Spenser doesn't seem to be part of our casual reading, like Shakespeare and Milton. This may be partly the fault of the editors, who have persistently kept the difficult spelling although they modernize all of his contemporaries. To some extent also it is the fault of critics who have claimed Spenser as a poet's poet and dwelt on qualities in his verse that are too precious for the common reader. In his own day, however, he was the plain man's poet as well. For more than a century *The Faerie Queene* was read by serious people as a source of ideas about life and conduct. Milton said that Spenser was a better teacher than Saint Thomas Aquinas, and he meant what he said.

We know what Spenser's plan for the poem was, because he explained it carefully in a letter addressed to his friend Sir Walter Raleigh. "The general end therefore of all the book is to fashion a gentleman or noble person in virtuous and gentle discipline." In each of twelve books there was to be a knight who represented a particular virtue, whose adventures would lead him into the various temptations that beset that virtue. He might fall into sin and even into very great danger, but always at the end he would emerge chastened yet triumphant. In each book there would also appear Prince Arthur, who represented the perfection of all the virtues.

When Spenser died he had published six books and written part of a seventh. It is possible that he had completed all twelve books, but if he had, the manuscripts were probably destroyed by fire. The first six virtues were these: Holiness, by which Spenser meant devotion to the true Christian faith; Temperance (moderation or self-control);

Chastity ("Britomartis, a lady Knight"); Friendship; Justice; and Courtesy.

Holiness, temperance, chastity, friendship, justice, courtesy. Not exactly a twentieth-century list. It is avowedly a list of *knightly* virtues, the qualities of a gentleman in Queen Elizabeth's court—Sir Philip Sidney or the Earl of Leicester or Sir Walter Raleigh spreading his cloak at the feet of his queen. No one in middle-class America sets out to earn his living by modeling himself on Sir Walter Raleigh. Yet consider these virtues by comparing them with their opposites. What are they, if not the qualities that the Nazi state has set out to abolish? It has declared explicitly that it will destroy religion, not simply some specific faith like Christianity or Judaism but all religion, faith, and worship or, as Spenser would say, holiness. Moderation is also marked for destruction. The Germans are the supermen, the master race, and outrageousness is the sign of their superiority. Chastity is meaningless in a country that commands all dutiful Nordics to breed children like cattle, more and more children for more and more battalions. Friendship? Only the alliance of men busy at the same kill. Hitler's friends learned what his friendship was worth one June night in 1934, and it is said that there is no one around him who calls him *du*. Justice? One of the delusions of the effete democracies. Courtesy? There are schools for training Nazi youth in the perfection of brutality, and the results of that training are written all over Europe.

We have all said repeatedly since this war began that the Nazi theory of morality is a denial of all the qualities that constitute civilized life. It is equally a denial of the qualities that Spenser combined in the portrait of a Christian gentleman, away back in the 1580's. In other words, in spite of differences in vocabulary and even greater differences in the structure of society, we are living under a code that has belonged to us for at least three centuries and a half, laid down even before Virginia was named for Queen Elizabeth or Jamestown for King James I.

Even in 1589 there was nothing new in such a catalogue of virtues, and Spenser was making no claim to originality when he chose them. In fact, the way he gathered his ideas from all sources is one of the most characteristically English things about the poem. English ideas have come from as many sources as the English peoples themselves, and one of the distinguishing traits of English literature has been its habit of gathering material from other literatures and re-working it for its own ends. Spenser tells us that he had the Aristotelian virtues in mind, and at least three of his virtues do come straight from Aristotle, though with a Christian difference. I imagine that if he had completed the poem he would have added at least three more from Aristotle's list—courage, liberality, and truthfulness.

Spenser's avowed master, of course, was Chaucer. In fact, a good place to start the pursuit of American ideas is Chaucer's Prologue to *The Canterbury Tales*. Chaucer died in 1400, and the Prologue is generally dated 1386. On an April morning, as practically everybody knows, nine-and-twenty pilgrims set out from the Tabard Inn in Southwark to go ahorse and afoot on a pilgrimage to Canterbury. Chaucer had chatted with them all the night before, got acquainted with them individually, and found out what business they were in—a very American procedure, if I may say so. In the Prologue he describes his twenty-nine pilgrims,

And at a Knight than wol I first beginne.

The Knight, as we perceive whenever he is mentioned, was very dear to Chaucer's heart. His virtues were the virtues of chivalry—truth and honor, liberality and courtesy. He had fought all over the heathen and Christian world—incidentally, in Russia, Prussia, and North Africa. He had always been reckoned a good soldier, but not the kind of soldier who is nourished on *Mein Kampf*. He never uttered any rudeness in all his life to any sort of person. He was "a verray, parfit gentil knight."

It is interesting to see how the same combination of virtues persists all down the centuries. Particularly it is interesting to see how the ideas of courtesy and friendliness and gentleness come down hand in hand with the virtues of both soldier and man of affairs. Nazi propaganda has announced repeatedly that the highest form of manhood is the soldier, but none of the Nazi glorifications of the soldier dwell upon his courtesy and gentleness.

In the century after Chaucer, William Caxton, obviously a very competent and American sort of person, introduced printing into England. With characteristically American motives he printed both books that people would like and books that would be good for them. He translated and printed among other things an *Art of Chivalry*, or knight's handbook, in which the twelve chivalric virtues are set down as nobleness, faith, loyalty, honor, uprightness, prowess, love, courtesy, diligence, cleanness, generosity, and soberness. I wonder if Spenser would have included diligence in his list; it is certainly one of the characteristic virtues of the English-speaking world today.

Spenser wrote about real men, too. He seems to have had a great capacity for personal admiration, and during his lifetime he had some very noble men to admire. One of his friends was Sir Philip Sidney, dead before *The Faerie Queene* ever saw light, with whom he seems to have had many earnest conversations about poetry and virtue. I might quote a description of Sidney from a nineteenth-century historian, John Richard Green.

Sidney, the nephew of Lord Leicester, was the idol of his time, and perhaps no figure reflects the age more fully and more beautifully. Fair as he was brave, quick of wit as of affection, noble and generous in temper, dear to Elizabeth as to Spenser, the darling of the court and of the camp, his learning and his genius made him the centre of the literary world which was springing into birth on English soil. . . . He flung away his life to save the English army in Flanders, and as he lay dying they brought a cup of water to his fevered lips. He bade them give it to a soldier who was stretched on the ground beside him. "Thy necessity," he said, "is greater than mine."

Another of Spenser's friends was Sir Walter Raleigh—soldier, adventurer, colonist, historian, poet, and courtier. Spenser's patron was the Earl of Leicester, whom he put into his poem as Prince Arthur, the pattern of all the virtues. In Ireland Spenser served under Lord Grey of Wilton, whom he put into his Fifth Book as the knight of justice. It was men like these who made England great in the great days of Elizabeth, altogether a rather splendid list of people for a poet to have lived with.

I open my Shakespeare and find men like these. Mark Antony says of Brutus:

> His life was gentle, and the elements
> So mixed in him that Nature might stand up
> And say to all the world, "This was a man!"

Bassanio says of Antonio:

> The dearest friend to me, the kindest man,
> The best-conditioned and unwearied spirit
> In doing courtesies, and one in whom
> The ancient Roman honor more appears
> Than any that draws breath in Italy.

Henry IV describes Hal:

> He hath a tear for pity, and a hand
> Open as day for melting charity.

It would be interesting to trace the process by which the aristocratic virtues of knighthood became the virtues of the middle classes in a commercial society. Addison and Steele played no small part in that development. Sir Roger de Coverley, the country baronet, and Sir Andrew Freeport, merchant and city knight, drank coffee together at the same club, and Sir Andrew's native goodness and good sense out-weighed any deficiency in courtly breeding. Bound volumes of *The Tatler* and *The Spectator* came to America with every consignment of books throughout the eighteenth century and were among the best read books of the merchants and lawyers and farmers of the New World. The eighteenth century saw also the beginnings of the novel, and one could fill a chapter with brave and courteous gentlemen from Fielding down through Scott and Thackeray to Galsworthy and our own day.

The tradition has come down in poetry as well. I might round out this chapter with two poems about real men, first the lines that Kipling wrote in memory of his American brother-in-law and, second, Vachel Lindsay's praise of a farmer whom he knew in Indiana. Both poems show how a conception of human nature can have its roots in times long past and yet belong to its own time and place as well, and how a character may be at once American and English.

To these who are cleansed of base Desire, Sorrow and Lust
    and Shame—
Gods for they knew the hearts of men, men for they stooped
    to Fame—
Borne on the breath that men call Death, my brother's
    spirit came.

He scarce had need to doff his pride or slough the dross
    of Earth—
E'en as he trod that day to God so walked he from his birth—
In simpleness and gentleness and honour and clean mirth.

So cup to lip in fellowship they gave him welcome high
And made him place at the banquet board—the Strong Men
    ranged thereby,
Who had done his work and held his peace and had
    no fear to die.

Lindsay's poem is called "The Proud Farmer," and these are the first, third, fourth, and final stanzas.

Into the acres of the newborn state
He poured his strength, and plowed his ancient name,
And, when the traders followed him, he stood
Towering above their furtive souls and tame.

He lived with liberal hand, and guests from far,
With talk and joke and fellowship to spare,—
Watching the wide world's life from sun to sun,
Lining his walls with books from everywhere.

He read by night, he built his world by day.
The farm and house of God to him were one.
For forty years he preached and ploughed and wrought—
A statesman in the fields, who bent to none.

And many a sturdy grandchild hears his name
In reverence spoken, till he feels akin
To all the lion-eyed who built the world—
And lion-dreams begin to burn within.

I should like to add three stanzas from an American poem
of this war, "The Drill," by Harry Brown. Although it is
less specific than the others, it gives, to me at least, a sense
of the presence of the same qualities, of the simpleness and
gentleness and honor of ordinary men.

The platoon moves past me into the mists of summer
And disappears into the darkness of our time,
A body of men, none known, none recognized,
Crossing my road for a little space. They go
Into the sun and the summer and the waiting war.

Seen for an instant and gone. Yet I felt between us
A bond not of country but of faith and love,
And I thought of an old phrase: "Whither thou goest,
I will go." And it seemed that the summer morning
Spoke out in a voice like a song, that the air was full of singing.

And something said, "They come and they go away,
The patient and the small. They go away into the sun,
Their names are forgotten and their few works also,
But when they go they take their weapons with them,
And they leave behind them houses heavy with honor."

III   Liberty and the Tradition

Give me liberty to know, to think, to believe, and to utter freely, according to conscience, above all other liberties.

JOHN MILTON, *Areopagitica*

What constitutes a State?
Not high-raised battlement or labored mound,
   Thick wall or moated gate;
Not cities fair, with spires and turrets crowned:
   No!—Men, high-minded men, . . .
   Men who their duties know,
But know their rights, and knowing, dare maintain;
   Prevent the long-aimed blow
And crush the tyrant, while they rend the chain.

ALCAEUS, *The State,* TRANSLATED BY SIR WILLIAM JONES

O star of morning and of liberty!
   O bringer of the light whose splendor shines
   Above the darkness of the Apennines,
Forerunner of the day that is to be!

HENRY WADSWORTH LONGFELLOW (TO DANTE),
Divina Commedia, SONNET VI

First, the people of the colonies are descendants of Englishmen. England, Sir, is a nation which still, I hope, respects, and formerly adored, her freedom. The colonists emigrated from you when this part of your character was most predominant, and they took this bias and direction the moment they parted from your hands. They are therefore not only devoted to liberty, but to liberty according to English ideas and on English principles.

EDMUND BURKE, On Conciliation with the Colonies

> We must be free or die, who speak the tongue
> That Shakespeare spake; the faith and morals hold
> Which Milton held.

WILLIAM WORDSWORTH, It Is Not to Be Thought Of

> Yet, Freedom! yet thy banner, torn, but flying,
> Streams like the thunder-storm against the wind.

GEORGE GORDON, LORD BYRON, Childe Harold's Pilgrimage

> Press on! the triumph shall be won
> Of common rights and equal laws,
> The glorious dream of Harrington,
> And Sidney's good old cause.

JOHN GREENLEAF WHITTIER, To the
Reformers of England

> All men shall be priests and kings,
> One royal brotherhood, one church made free
> By love, which is the law of liberty!

JOHN GREENLEAF WHITTIER, Garibaldi

God grant that not only the love of liberty but a thorough knowledge of the rights of man may pervade all the nations of the earth, so that a philosopher may set his foot anywhere on its surface and say: This is my country.

BENJAMIN FRANKLIN

"Let a great Assembly be
Of the fearless and the free,
On some spot of English ground
Where the plains stretch wide around.

"Let the blue sky overhead,
The green earth on which ye tread,
All that must eternal be,
Witness the solemnity.

. . . .

"Let a vast Assembly be,
And with great solemnity
Declare with measured words that ye
Are, as God has made ye, free!"

PERCY BYSSHE SHELLEY, *The Mask of Anarchy*

. . . . The pulse of England still beats slowly; undeterred, for there are things there that cannot be destroyed. Only the bodies of free men and women can be destroyed. The bodies of free men and women easily, but not their minds which are steadfast. Nor can the sap of the broken trees be stopped from running, nor the seeds in pitted fields from germinating.
Should the dark cloud fall, should our island be destroyed there will be no finality in that destruction, for the seed of England is too widely sown, too deeply planted. The death of old England cannot destroy her spawn, nor the rasing of her monuments undo the charters of her justice.

STUART CLOETE, . . . *Of England*

Not long ago I read an editorial about another editorial on "a government of laws and not of men." The second editor seemed to think that this was a novel and admirable phrase, embodying his own ideas about liberty under law. In point of fact, however, the phrase is far from new. It comes out of the preamble to the constitution of the Commonwealth of Massachusetts, and the men who placed it there in the eighteenth century got it from a seventeenth-century Englishman, one Algernon Sidney, and even he did not claim that the idea was new.

It is in some such way, almost invariably, that American ideas have come down to us. I do not say this for the sake of being irritating but because for me it is a pleasant and comfortable thought. Many people, I have discovered, feel outraged by the suggestion that American political ideas were frequently thought up first by somebody else in another country. They like to believe that constitutional government, the Bill of Rights, and political freedom in general all sprang up fully armed on American soil. I can only say that my feeling is entirely different. I cannot see why we should wish to have discovered democracy any more than poetry or religion or any other good thing. For a person of my temperament the long ancestry of our ideas is in itself a kind of guarantee of their virtue.

I feel more or less as Newman did about the Catholic Church: *Quod semper, quod ubique, quod ab omnibus creditum est, justum et securum est.* Our creed has not been believed always, everywhere, and by all men, I admit, but it has been believed for a long time, in a great many places, by a great many people. Political faiths, like religions, have their goodly fellowships of prophets and their noble armies of martyrs. As Walt Whitman said,

> Not a grave of the murder'd for freedom but
> grows seed for freedom, in its turn to
> bear seed,
> Which the winds carry afar and re-sow, and
> the rains and the snows nourish.

I like to think that our seed has come from England and Italy and Greece and Judea. I like to think we have learned lessons of liberty from every country that has sent us its sons or its books. I like to think we are still learning.

I have not the scholarship to trace the development of American institutions from the historian's point of view. As usual, I am thinking of the books that lie behind the history, whether they are argument first and literature second, like Locke's essays on government, or literature pure and simple, like Addison's *Cato*. I once spent several months looking for literary-political references in eighteenth-century New England, chiefly in newspapers and sermons. My research made no great contribution to knowledge; in fact, I don't think it benefited anyone except myself, but I know that I learned a great deal. I still vividly remember, for instance, the cumulative effect of innumerable booksellers' advertisements listing consignments of books from England. It is a mistake to suppose that our Puritan ancestors spent their time poring over *Pilgrim's Progress* and Foxe's *Book of Martyrs*. They were much more likely to be digging into Harrington or Algernon Sidney or Locke. The booksellers' lists have *Locke on Civil Government, Locke on Toleration, The Tatler* and *The Spectator, Addison's Cato, Montesquieu on the Spirit of the Laws,* and always Locke, Locke, and more Locke. In the election-day sermons he almost completely displaced the Apostle Paul. It is interesting to reflect how for decades English political theory must have been disseminated in this country by practically nameless men—preachers, lawyers, and editors of embryonic newspapers.

One almost forgotten source of political inspiration is Addison's *Cato*. The story of its first production is often told as one of the amusing yarns of dramatic history. In the last days of Queen Anne the problem of her successor became increasingly acute. Parliament in the Act of Settlement had designated the Electress Sophia of Hanover and her heirs, and the Whigs were bound to support this succession as both constitutional and Protestant. On the other hand, there wasn't the ghost of a chance of arousing any personal enthusiasm for German George, and there was real danger of a revival of Tory loyalty to the exiled Stuarts and the Divine Right of Kings. The Whig leaders were hard put to it to rekindle the old hatred of Stuart tyranny. It came to their ears that Mr. Addison had an unfinished play that might be turned to good advantage. It was a play of ancient Rome, full of liberty, patriotism, and defiance of tyrants. If it could be made clear that liberty and patriotism belonged to the Whigs and tyranny to the Tories, it would be a splendid piece of propaganda.

The play was finished, the night came, and the audience was packed with Whigs, all primed to applaud the Whig virtues of patriotism and liberty while the Tories sat in embarrassed silence. Unfortunately for the scheme, the secret leaked out and the Tory camp came prepared to outdo the Whigs in frenzied applause. Between the acts the Tory minister called the chief actor into his box and presented him with a purse of gold for so nobly portraying the *Tory* virtues. No wonder the play was a success!

What is more remarkable is that it remained a popular play throughout the century for readers even more than for playgoers. Its noble speeches were learned by heart, and many of its lines became familiar quotations. It must have been in gentlemen's libraries all up and down the Atlantic seaboard, and it is known to have been one of Thomas Jefferson's favorite books. It is the story of Marcus Porcius Cato in the last days of the Roman republic, making a noble but hopeless stand against the dictatorship of Julius Caesar.

> Greatly unfortunate, he fights the cause
> Of honor, virtue, liberty, and Rome.

The armies draw closer to Cato's city and Caesar makes flattering overtures, but never for a moment does Cato consider appeasing the tyrant.

> A day, an hour, of virtuous liberty
> Is worth a whole eternity in bondage.
>
> . . . .
>
> The hand of fate is over us, and heav'n
> Exacts severity from all our thoughts:
> It is not now a time to talk of aught
> But chains or conquest, liberty or death.

If you look up Patrick Henry's speech, you will find that chains and slavery are there along with liberty and death.

> Remember, O my friends, the laws, the rights,
> The generous plan of power delivered down,
> From age to age, by your renowned forefathers,
> (So dearly bought, the price of so much blood)
> Oh, let it never perish in your hands!
> But piously transmit it to your children.
> Do thou, great Liberty, inspire our souls,
> And make our lives in thy possession happy,
> Or our deaths glorious in thy just defense.

The lines seem stilted enough as we read them today, but two centuries ago they stirred men's blood and rang out as watchwords of the American Revolution.

It was one of the blessings of the classical curriculum that it made boys read Greek and Roman history during their impressionable years. The stories of republican Rome, from Horatius at the bridge to the conspiracy of Brutus and Cassius, became an integral part of the British and American mind. For Shakespeare, Brutus was the noblest Roman of them all. The story of Cato, as we said before, became involved in constitutional history, the Hanoverian succession, and eventually the American Revolution. Macaulay's *Lays of Ancient Rome* turned out to be full of good Roman Whigs. Taking it all in all, the republicanism of Rome seems to have been domesticated in the English-speaking mind from the Renaissance on.

Greek history is perhaps less British but much more exciting. Here you have not only the development of demo-

31

cratic institutions but the fight of the free city states against mighty aggressors—against the apparently invincible power of Persia in the fifth century B.C. and the truly invincible power of Macedon in the fourth. There was a time when Marathon and Thermopylae were part of every high school curriculum, and they were good food for the growing soul.

In the fall of 1941 when Italy and Germany invaded Greece, these stories began to be retold. In 490 B.C. the Emperor Darius sent an army of one hundred thousand Persians to invade Greece from the north. Ten thousand Athenians and one thousand Plataeans met the invading army on the plain of Marathon and defeated it. The Greeks lost one hundred and ninety-two men and the Persians more than six thousand. The runner Pheidippides carried the message from Marathon to Athens, "Rejoice, we conquer," and fell dead in the market place. Ten years later Xerxes, the son of Darius, sent a second and mightier army. The position of the Greeks was betrayed, and Leonidas and his band held the pass of Thermopylae while the main army withdrew. Three hundred Spartans and seven hundred Thespians fought to the last man. "O stranger," wrote the Greek poet Simonides, in lines of great simplicity and power, "tell the Lacedaemonians that we lie here obedient to their commands."

Obedient also to the idea of liberty, and destined to become a symbol of the fight for freedom. More than two thousand years later Byron traveled in Greece and made his way to the famous battlefields. They recur in his poetry again and again, from "Childe Harold" to "Don Juan."

> The mountains look on Marathon—
> And Marathon looks on the sea;
> And musing there an hour alone,
> I dreamed that Greece might still be free;
> For standing on the Persians' grave,
> I could not deem myself a slave.

. . . .

Must *we* but weep o'er days more blest?
Must *we* but blush?—Our fathers bled.
Earth! render back from out thy breast
A remnant of our Spartan dead!
Of the three hundred grant but three,
To make a new Thermopylae!

"Thus sung, or would, or could, or should have sung, the modern Greek, in tolerable verse." Byron sang about Greece, and also, as everyone knows, gave his fortune, his very considerable practical abilities, and finally his life to the cause of Greek freedom. When he died at Missolonghi in 1824, the Greek revolution looked like a gallant failure, but his dying did Greece more good than anything else he could have done. His poetry and his death together played a real part in exciting the popular enthusiasm that brought England into the war on the side of Greece. I suppose you could say that the heroism of ancient Greece, transmitted by the English system of education and revivified by the genius of a liberty-loving poet, was combined with the heroism of modern Greece to put a new free nation on the map of Europe.

I ponder how from Attic seed
There grew an English tree,
How Byron like his heroes fell,
Fighting a country free,
And Swinburne took from Shelley's lips
The kiss of Poetry.

The poet who wrote those lines, James Elroy Flecker, died of tuberculosis in 1915, seeing in the First World War another chapter in the history and poetry of freedom. You could make a good anthology of the poetry of freedom and call it "From Byron to Spender." It would be full of gloriously defiant heroes, resisting tyrant invaders and overthrowing tyranny at home. Byron, Shelley, and Swinburne would all be in the table of contents; Browning for single passages, though rarely for whole poems; Whittier, Lowell,

33

Emerson, and Walt Whitman, besides men whom we should have forgotten entirely if they hadn't written single poems like "Arnold von Winkelried" and "Marco Bozzaris."

It is interesting, I think, to see how all these nineteenth-century poets seized upon the fight for freedom wherever they found it. They made the fall of the Bastille and the battles of Concord and Lexington and Marathon and Thermopylae all part of the same great saga. English poets very early put their faith in the new American republic and accepted Washington as the type-hero of a free people. All the revolutions and all the revolutionaries had their poets.

> A glorious people vibrated again
> The lightning of the Nations; Liberty,
> From heart to heart, from tower to tower, o'er Spain
> Scattering contagious fire into the sky . . .

So Shelley wrote in 1819.

> The world's great age begins anew,
>   The golden years return,
> The earth doth like a snake renew
>   Her winter weeds outworn:
> Heaven smiles, and faiths and empires gleam,
> Like wrecks of a dissolving dream.

So he wrote of the revolution in Greece in 1822. To his ardent spirit it seemed that the triumph of freedom would bring all other blessings in its train.

As the century went on, the list of revolutions lengthened, and with it the list of heroes: Bozzaris, Mazzini, Garibaldi, Kossuth, Bolívar. The poets themselves became symbols of the same struggle.

> Shakespeare was of us, Milton was for us,
>   Burns, Shelley, were with us,—they watch
>   from their graves!

Victor Hugo was a hero to Swinburne because of the part he played in the Revolution of 1848. Walt Whitman was another of Swinburne's heroes because his seemed the clearest voice of the American republic.

> Send but a song oversea for us,
>   Heart of their hearts who are free,
> Heart of their singer, to be for us
>   More than our singing can be.

The history of freedom is a history of emotions, and emotions live more by symbols than by logic. It is a piece of literary history that the poets started glorifying freedom at just about the same time that they fell in love with nature. They found liberty in all the great free forms of nature—mountains, oceans, west winds. There is a characteristic quatrain in Emerson's "Monadnoc"; very bad poetry, I am afraid, but typical.

> To myself I oft recount
> Tales of many a famous mount,—
> Wales, Scotland, Uri, Hungary's dells:
> Bards, Roys, Scanderbegs, and Tells.

Heroes and mountains crowd into his mind together, faster than the octosyllabics can handle them—the Welsh bard of Gray's poem who cursed the invading English, the outlaw Rob Roy in the Trossachs, Schiller's Wilhelm Tell leading the four forest cantons of Switzerland, Scanderbeg (who was a hero for Longfellow as well) "fighting a country free" among his mountains. Emerson might also have remembered Shelley's lines to Mont Blanc:

> Thou hast a voice, great Mountain, to repeal
> Large codes of fraud and woe.

Certainly he knew Wordsworth's sonnet on the subjugation of Switzerland.

> Two voices are there; one is of the sea,
> One of the mountains; each a mighty Voice:
> In both from age to age thou didst rejoice,
> They were thy chosen music, Liberty!

35

One critic of Wordsworth has warned us against thinking of Wordsworth as writing "nature poetry." Not nature
poetry, he says, but "a medicine for the soul." I think the
injunction holds good for all the poets that I am putting
into this chapter. These mountains and winds and oceans
are medicines, tonics, stimulants for a sick world. We mis-
understand the Romantics altogether if we turn these things
into sedatives.

> Will they tie the winds in a tether,
>   Put a bit in the jaws of the sea?
> While three men hold together,
>   The kingdoms are less by three.
>
> . . . .
>
> All the world has its burdens to bear,
>   From Cayenne to the Austrian whips;
> Forth, with the rain in our hair
>   And the salt sweet foam in our lips;
>
> In the teeth of the hard glad weather,
>   In the blown wet face of the sea;
> While three men hold together
>   The kingdoms are less by three.

This "Song in Time of Order," I suppose, was one of the
poems Flecker remembered when he thought of Shelley and
Swinburne together. The "Ode to the West Wind," if you
really look at it, is a prayer of a poet of freedom.

> Drive my dead thoughts over the universe
> Like withered leaves to quicken a new birth!

It would be a joy to Shelley if he could know that his
wild west wind is still blowing through American poetry,
in lines like the ones that Genevieve Taggard wrote for
Mallorca.

> O wild west wind . . . Liberty's open roar,
> Blow on this island, blow the ocean clean,
> Drown our tormentors, blow equinox, blow war

Away from the world. Drive to us the unseen
Battalions, clouds of planes by workers flown,
Give us our land again, quiet and green,

Our children singing and our land, our own
Ways, our wives, our delegates. Blow here.

It is time, I think, to turn from poetry to prose, from
Shelley and Swinburne to Jefferson and Burke, and this
brings me to one more aspect of the development of the
tradition. It has been characteristic of us to single out, at
one time or another, one particular practical issue on which
to focus all our attention. Burke makes this point in his
defense of the American colonies. "Liberty inheres in some
sensible object," he says, "and every nation has formed to
itself some favorite point, which by way of eminence becomes the criterion of their happiness. It happened you
know, Sir, that the great contests for freedom in this country were from the earliest times chiefly upon the question
of taxing." He goes on in a long paragraph to summarize
the development of that fundamental principle, the right of
a free people to vote its own taxes. "The colonists draw
from you, as with their life-blood, these ideas and principles. Their love of liberty, as with you, fixed and attached
on this special point of taxing." That is to say, for centuries
taxation was the foremost of symbols. Taxation imposed
was tyranny; taxation freely voted meant liberty.

This was certainly true of eighteenth-century America.
I am inclined to think that in the nineteenth century the
emotional emphasis shifted and the chief symbol became
not the right to tax but the right to vote. Manhood suffrage
came early and rather easily in America; later in England,
after much controversy and bitterness. The Fourteenth
Amendment gave suffrage to the liberated slaves and strictly
enjoined any state from refusing that right (with penalties
that have never been enforced). The right to vote was the
symbol of freedom.

In the campaign that culminated in the Nineteenth Amendment the vote was again a symbol and aroused an intensity of emotion that far exceeded its practical benefits. Sensible people looked at women clamoring for the vote and said, "What good is it going to do them?" Just the same question that the Tories asked when the colonies demanded the right to tax themselves, and the answer was the same: When one single right becomes the symbol of all the other rights, then it must be secured at any cost, or freedom is lost. In recent months the right to vote has been twice a matter of controversy, once in the argument over the machinery of the soldiers' vote and again in the proposal to abolish the poll tax in federal elections. In other democracies, in other times and places, these problems might be negligible. For us, as our tradition has developed in the last hundred years, they stand at the very heart of the democratic faith. It is by controversies such as these that the Rights of Man have been transformed, sometimes all too slowly, from glittering generalities into solid, meaningful facts.

Although it may not be obvious, I am now coming round in a circle to the idea with which I started this chapter—that it is a good thing to regard American political ideas as part of a long and growing tradition. You will recall that I used the word *comfortable*. I can put more confidence in a gradual accretion than in a single revelation. Liberty is not the kind of thing that exists perfect, ideal, and unvarying, like the square on the hypotenuse of a right triangle. On the contrary, it is known only as it is experienced by actual people under specific circumstances, at a definite time and place.

Our principles and practices have come to us from many sources, and they have had to be adapted to a great variety of conditions, and they still survive. They are not right because certain people promulgated them on the Atlantic seaboard in the 1700's; they are right because they are *right* —in the world today. In fact, as I read newspapers and listen to speeches, it seems to me that too great insistence on the authority of the founders of the Republic has become a dangerous thing. People argue: "This is what Jefferson said, so it must be right," or "Jefferson never said this, so it must be wrong." No arguments of this sort carry weight in the light of the greater tradition. There are many Jeffersonian ideas that Jefferson never thought of. The ideas of American democracy do not rest upon any single authority, and they cannot be destroyed by any single attack.

Moreover, I find that a consciousness of the tradition carries with it great hope for the future. It reminds us that all good things come slowly. The growth of all these ideas, in all these countries, has been slow. It is by slow processes that they have become acceptable to large bodies of men, and by still slower processes that they have been put into operation. As I write we do not yet know whether or not this present Congress will abolish the poll tax laws and enfranchise another large group of native-born Americans. Even if there is still another delay, the tradition assures us that our course is steadily toward a just and uniform suffrage and will not be stayed.

Looking at the future, we can hope not only that the rights we have inherited will be more perfectly assured but that new ones will be added. Our present rights have been won successively and not simultaneously. The point at issue has been sometimes taxation, sometimes resistance to external tyranny, sometimes the suffrage, sometimes equality before the law. None of the men who drew up the great democratic documents of earlier centuries had a complete notion of liberty and democracy as we understand them today. Trusting the evidence of the tradition, we can expect that many proposals that outrage conservative minds today will work themselves into the fabric of our government and

39

become as respectable as the Declaration of Independence.
Give them time.

All in all, the more I study the democratic tradition, the
greater cause I see for faith and hope. That tradition goes
back through so many centuries, it has gathered strength
from so many sources, it has found itself so many symbols.
It has aroused, it still arouses, such passionate devotion. If
the specific failures of democracy are many—and they are—
so are the failures of every other form of government about
which we have any information. In the last hundred and
fifty years no country under any other system of government can match the democratic countries in steadfast progress, in the destruction of evil and the establishment of
good. Even in the catastrophes of this present war, no
country that has lived long in the democratic faith has
turned to any other political gospel for its salvation.

IV   *Of Goodness*

And what doth the Lord require of thee, but to do justly,
and to love mercy, and to walk humbly with thy God?

MICAH

Let us now praise famous men and our fathers that
begot us.   ECCLESIASTICUS

"Let us now praise famous men"—
  Men of little showing—
For their work continueth,
And their work continueth,
Broad and deep continueth,
  Greater than their knowing!

RUDYARD KIPLING, *A School Song*

There is
One great society alone on earth:
The noble Living and the noble Dead.

WILLIAM WORDSWORTH, *The Prelude*

His was no lonely mountain-peak of mind,
Thrusting to thin air o'er our cloudy bars,
A sea-mark now, now lost in vapors blind;
Broad prairie rather, genial, level-lined,
Fruitful and friendly for all human kind,
Yet also nigh to heaven and loved of loftiest stars. . . .

An American Credo

Our children shall behold his fame,
  The kindly-earnest, brave, foreseeing man,
Sagacious, patient, dreading praise, not blame,
  New birth of our new soil, the first American.

JAMES RUSSELL LOWELL'S DESCRIPTION OF LINCOLN, IN
Ode Recited at the Harvard Commemoration

Our yeoman should be equal to his home
Set in the fair, green valleys, purple walled,
A man to match his mountains, not to creep
Dwarfed and abased below them.

JOHN GREENLEAF WHITTIER, *Among the Hills*

Love virtue, she alone is free,
She can teach ye how to climb
Higher than the sphery chime;
Or if virtue feeble were,
Heaven itself would stoop to her.

JOHN MILTON, *Comus*

Geoffrey Chaucer, poet, idealist, burgher of London, Commissioner of Dykes and Ditches, who loved his fellow-men, both good and bad, and found no answer to the puzzle of life but in truth and courage and beauty and belief in God.

GEORGE LYMAN KITTREDGE, *Chaucer and His Poetry*

NONE CAN love freedom heartily but good men; the rest love not freedom, but license." That was Milton's opinion, and he had thought much about both freedom and goodness. It is reasonable also to say that none but good men can constitute a free society or, perhaps more accu-

42

rately, that a free society can succeed only when a considerable number of its citizens are good men. In a study of any democracy it is pertinent to consider both its theories and its habits of goodness.

Here in America it would be interesting if we could have a poll that would show how we estimate the relative importance of different virtues. Of the four so-called cardinal virtues—prudence, temperance, justice, and fortitude—I imagine that fortitude would rank highest and temperance lowest. Justice would be pretty well up. Of the three Christian virtues—faith, hope, and charity—I should guess that the last would be first and the middle one still middle. Some of the virtues of the Beatitudes might not come out very well. Meekness, for instance. "Blessed are the meek" has never been a favorite American text. The stock of the peacemakers has fluctuated a good deal lately. On the whole, perhaps, we incline to be dubious about the people who hunger and thirst after righteousness. I remember that as a child I took *after* in the temporal sense and imagined that the people of the Fourth Beatitude had been righteous so strenuously that they needed a good square meal afterward. Many other people, I have observed, regard righteousness as somewhat exhausting and not to be practiced too freely. And how do we feel about the pure in heart?

As for simple goodness, I should not be surprised if we got quite a substantial negative vote. Of course a lot depends on how you word your question. It has been pointed out that you could get a vote in favor of the common cold by asking, "Would you be willing to catch cold to kiss Hedy Lamarr?" You could get a vote against butter by asking, "Would you eat butter to please Hitler?" If you asked baldly, "Do you believe in goodness?" I firmly believe that many people would say no. Then they would make speeches. One man would start on a diatribe against self-righteousness. Another would say that goodness was

43

lackadaisical, that he liked somebody with guts enough to
be a good sinner. He might quote the epitaph for Mary
Jones—"no hits, no runs, no errors"—which, after all, is only
a twentieth-century rendering of Milton's great sentence,
"I cannot praise a fugitive and cloistered virtue, unexercised
and unbreathed, that never sallies out and sees her adversary." A third man would be purely personal. "I've had
enough goodness for a lifetime. X was a good man, and of
all the dirty, double-crossing skunks . . . !" I think all
these responses are American, and I'm not at all sure that
they do not indicate rather healthy states of mind.

One thing we obviously need is a definition of goodness.
We might look at Bacon's essay "Of Goodness and Goodness of Nature." "I take Goodness," he says, "in this sense,
the affecting [we should say *aiming at* or *desiring*] of the
weal of men, which is that the Grecians call *Philanthropia*.
. . . Goodness answers to the theological virtue Charity,
and admits no excess." "Admits no excess"; that is to say,
cannot be had in too great quantities. That was the meaning of goodness that you were likely to find in Bacon's
century. There was a distinction between righteousness,
which consisted in doing right, and goodness, which consisted in doing good. The Son of Man went about doing
good. Goodness was active, positive, practical, and kind.
Righteousness might be cold and dead, but goodness was
warm, human, alive. We have come to use the word goodness today for a negative quality that is even less attractive
than righteousness, and we have not added any new word
to take the place of the one we have spoiled. Maybe we
shall some day, when we realize that we need it.

You still hear the old usage sometimes. We say, "Isn't
that good of him!" when we mean that somebody, out of
the goodness of his heart (we still use that phrase, though
we often use it ironically) has done something positively
and practically and perhaps unnecessarily kind. When I

was a child there was an elderly gentleman in my town of whom I knew only two things, that he was rich and that he was good. How he got his money I never thought to inquire. I rather think he inherited it. He never seemed to do anything with it except spend it. He made up the deficit in the minister's salary and paid for the janitor's wife's operation. He paid back the money that somebody's boy stole from the butcher and got the boy another job and kept him straight. Some of our nice old ladies let him pay for the little comforts that their economies could never have managed. (They promised not to tell.) People in trouble went to him. When he died, families who had never asked for help in their lives said to each other, "Who shall we go to now? We always knew he was there if we needed him."

One of the deacons of our most strait-laced congregation walked home with my father after the funeral. He shook his head sorrowfully. It was a pity, he said, that such a good man as Mr. Gates should have to go to Hell. "Yes," said my father, "it *would* be."

Now that kind of goodness, at any rate, I think we believe in. If we believe in Heaven, we believe that Mr. Gates is the sort of person who goes there. If we believe in the Gospels, we like reading the explicit statement in the twenty-fifth chapter of Matthew, when the King says to those on his right hand, "Come, ye blessed of my Father, inherit the kingdom prepared for you from the foundation of the world."

For I was hungry, and ye gave me to eat; I was thirsty, and ye gave me drink; I was a stranger, and ye took me in; naked, and ye clothed me, . . .

Then shall the righteous answer him, saying, Lord, when saw we thee hungry, and fed thee? or athirst, and gave thee drink? . . .

And the King shall answer and say unto them, Verily I say unto you, Inasmuch as ye did it unto one of these my brethren, even these least, ye did it unto me.

45

Do you know "A Lyke-Wake Dirge"? I met it first in *The Oxford Book of English Verse*. It can't very well be quoted except in the old spelling.

> This ae nighte, this ae nighte,
>   —*Every nighte and alle,*
> Fire and sleet and candle-lighte,
>   *And Christe receive thy saule.*
>
> When thou from hence away art past,
>   —*Every nighte and alle,*
> To Whinny-muir thou com'st at last;
>   *And Christe receive thy saule.*
>
> If ever thou gavest hosen and shoon,
>   —*Every nighte and alle,*
> Sit thee down and put them on:
>   *And Christe receive thy saule.*
>
> If hosen and shoon thou ne'er gav'st nane
>   —*Every nighte and alle,*
> The whinnes sall prick thee to the bare bane;
>   *And Christe receive thy saule.*
>
> . . . .
>
> If ever thou gavest meat or drink,
>   —*Every nighte and alle,*
> The fire sall never make thee shrink;
>   *And Christe receive thy saule.*
>
> . . . .
>
> This ae nighte, this ae nighte,
>   —*Every nighte and alle,*
> Fire and sleet and candle-lighte,
>   *And Christe receive thy saule.*

It isn't a question of being good in order to get to heaven. One kind of goodness that Americans tend to distrust is the kind that seems to have one eye always on rewards in the hereafter. No; it is simply that in this world there are some people who do good because they *are* good and then find out, often to their own surprise, that the

Lord is pleased with them. I always like to hear Marian Anderson sing "All God's Chillun Got Wings." The amount of meaning that she can put into "Ev'rybody talkin' 'bout heaven ain't goin' there" is worth ten sermons. Deep in your stomach you have a sudden conviction about the kind of goodness that counts.

I can see that this belief of ours, like so many others, has a varied ancestry. It belongs to us partly, as I suggested before, because it comes out of the Bible and Christian teaching. It is one of those Christian doctrines widely accepted also by people who do not profess and call themselves Christians. It belongs to us, too, because in the nineteenth century it went hand in hand with the doctrine of liberty. It may sound absurd to cite Byron as an apostle of virtue when his ordinary reputation is that of devil's disciple, yet actually one of the things Byron preached was the goodness of doing good.

It is typical of Byron's age that it chose Prometheus for a hero in a double role: he defied the tyranny of Jove, and he did good to men.

> Thy Godlike crime was to be kind,
> To render with thy precepts less
> The sum of human wretchedness,
> And strengthen Man with his own mind.

The *fraternité* of *liberté, égalité, fraternité* became *brotherhood* in English, which somehow seems to carry greater implications of practical kindliness. What Longfellow said of Burns is true of all the liberty-loving poets.

> But still the music of his song
> Rises o'er all, elate and strong;
> Its master-chords
> Are Manhood, Freedom, Brotherhood.

There were various points of morality on which Burns and Byron differed from the New Englanders, but on the com-

47

bination of freedom and brotherly goodness they were in perfect accord.

I think this kind of goodness is characteristically American; it throve naturally on the frontier, and it has kept on flourishing in places that the frontier has left behind. In a new community, cut off from the machinery of organized society, practical goodness becomes a necessary part of existence. Moreover, the natural impulses toward kindness and generosity are less inhibited by self-consciousness and custom. The frontier gave men, and more especially women, opportunities for indulging in the pleasures of goodness. I realize that, technically speaking, the frontier has been closed since 1890, but in many ways it still seems to lie round about us. I rather think that the so-called inconveniences of rationing have revived some of the relationships of earlier days and have afforded real comfort to people who like being good to each other.

Suppose we agree that Americans on the whole approve of goodness of this sort. If we went further, though, I imagine that we should find much greater uncertainty; there would be an increased percentage of votes in the category "No opinion." Let me go back to Spenser and *The Faerie Queene*. Spenser wasn't telling a young man how to *do* anything—how to succeed, how to get rich, how to make friends and influence people. He wasn't telling his readers what to do but what to be. Now we may say offhand that this is one of the silly things about the poem. It is un-American; Americans are doers. That is quite true. "Faith without works is dead" is a good American text, and the American faith in work and works demands a chapter to itself. On the other hand, maybe we are closer to Spenser than we realize. Maybe unconsciously we value achievements less than we think, and qualities of goodness more. We admit as much in our casual, half-slangy estimates of people. We say that So-and-so is a good egg, a good scout, a right guy, a guy you can trust, somebody to tie to. More than we think, we admire people, as Spenser did, for being what they are. It may be one of the deficiencies of the literature of this century that it hasn't made us see clearly enough what kind of people we believe in.

Why shouldn't someone write a modern *Faerie Queene* and call it *What Makes a Good Egg?* Which brings up another sense in which we use the word *good*. We speak of things as being good all the way through. It is notorious that there is no such thing as a partially good egg. An apple, to be sure, may be good in the spots where the worm hasn't yet arrived, but we still maintain a distinction between a good apple and a wormy one. There is a comparable quality in people, and I think we recognize it. This is what Bacon called "goodness of nature" in the essay I have quoted. There are men who by their natural make-up are good in all the senses of the word, and we like them that way. They do right and not wrong because their whole nature is averse to wrongdoing. There is in them a kind of substantial goodness that is satisfying, like good food or good weather.

We find a great deal of this intrinsic goodness in the literature of nineteenth-century America. In recent years it has been customary to disparage American writers, and the New Englanders in particular, for this very reason. We ascribe to them a narrow-minded morality that the best minds escaped entirely. The people who wrote stories of moral instruction for school readers were perhaps responsible for our present strong tendency to demand wickedness in literature and to assume that if a book is full of virtuous people, it must be bad. To be sure, it is both bad art and bad ethics to deny the existence of sins and sinners. No picture of life is complete that leaves out its manifold sins and wickedness, to say nothing of its hypocrisies and affectations. On the other hand I see no artistic objection

49

to accurate representations of goodness when goodness is what you see before you. A great deal of our nineteenth-century literature was pretty poor; nobody can deny it. But much of what these men wrote was better than we realize, and one of its qualities of excellence, I believe, is this very representation of goodness in people.

Emerson, Whittier, and Hawthorne, for instance, give us a consistent sense of their own goodness. Not intentionally, not with any self-righteousness; rather because their words are so clearly the voices of their souls and their souls are so clearly single and clean. There is a kind of primordial innocence about them, "still quiring to the young-eyed cherubins."

> So nigh is grandeur to our dust,
> So near is God to man . . .

Emerson seems to be talking about personal experience. He was conscious, too, of the goodness of men about him, of people like Longfellow. "The gentleman whose funeral we have been attending was a sweet and beautiful soul," he said in the vagueness that came upon him in old age, "but— I have forgotten his name."

In Longfellow's own poetry you get a constant sense of the friendship and fellowship of good men. He found them in his books and in real life. He was no Chaucer, don't mistake me. Even for good people he lacked some of Chaucer's zest, and of course he had no genius for creating a Nun's Priest or a Wife of Bath. It is no kindness to him to put the Prelude to the *Tales of a Wayside Inn* next to Chaucer's Prologue. The landlord, "known in all Sudbury as 'The Squire' " seems pale beside Harry Baillie. The student, who is compounded of Chaucer's clerk and one of Longfellow's friends and Longfellow himself, is a rather ethereal figure, but still worth putting into a poem.

> A youth was there, of quiet ways,
> A Student of old books and days,

To whom all tongues and lands were known,
And yet a lover of his own.

. . . .

Books were his passion and delight,
And in his upper room at home
Stood many a rare and sumptuous tome,
In vellum bound, with gold bedight,
Great volumes garmented in white,
Recalling Florence, Pisa, Rome.

The young Sicilian, the Spanish Jew from Alicant, the
Poet, all carry with them the breath of virtue. The Musi-
cian (Ole Bull, Longfellow said) had not only a Norwegian
beauty of face but "a radiance streaming from within."
And the Theologian, Wales or Channing or whoever he
was in real life, would have been no unworthy friend of
Chaucer's parson.

Skilful alike with tongue and pen,
He preached to all men everywhere
The Gospel of the Golden Rule.

. . . .

With reverent feet the earth he trod,
Nor banished nature from his plan,
But studied still with deep research
To build the Universal Church,
Lofty as is the love of God,
And ample as the wants of man.

If Longfellow lacked what Kittredge calls Chaucer's "stu-
pendous luck in always meeting nonpareils," he had his own
luck in meeting the pure in heart.

Certainly we have had later poets, too, who have main-
tained this same faith in good men. The growing list of
poems on Lincoln, as well as Carl Sandburg's great volumes
of prose, bear testimony to this faith. Vachel Lindsay and
Edwin Arlington Robinson and Robert Frost, to name only
three, have put their trust in human goodness. In fact, I
wonder if one great source of Frost's popularity does not

51

lie in a feeling he gives his readers that the poet himself is good to the core.

Yes, I suspect that America has produced even more than its fair share of good men, "the noble living and the noble dead" of Wordsworth's phrase. We have had our great good men in the grand manner, and along with them a nameless host whose simple, matter-of-fact goodness is also part of our heritage.

In fact, I am convinced that we take goodness too much for granted and that one of our national deficiencies is ignorance of evil. If, as I suggested earlier, our ideas of goodness are inconsistent and uncertain, in our theories of evil we are in a state of downright confusion.

I can make myself clearer if I turn once more to Milton, about whose theory of evil there was never any doubt. It is the backbone of *Paradise Lost*. Too many people today know the poem only from the first two books and have the mistaken notion that Satan is Milton's hero. On the contrary, for Milton the heart of the poem was in Books IV and IX, in which Satan was the unmistakable villain.

Let me say quite simply that the theme of *Paradise Lost* is the losing of Paradise, "Of Man's first disobedience, and the fruit of that forbidden tree. . . ." The hero of the poem is Adam. It was the eating of the fruit of the forbidden tree that "brought death into the world and all our woe." That is to say, the poem is about the fall of man and the origin of evil. If Satan is in the poem, he is there to explain evil, to explain why Adam fell and why Adam's descendants suffer. He invades the Garden of Eden in Book IV, he tempts Eve and thereby Adam in Book IX, he returns triumphant to Hell in Book X, to find that his triumph is a hissing and an abomination. From start to finish, Satan is the enemy, the arch plotter, the invader of neutral territory, the first political liar, the first anti-Semite, the first Nazi.

Let us see more precisely what Milton set out to say. In the first place, Satan was cast out of Heaven for pride and ambition. He was the first Fuehrer. He said to his angels, "We are the Herrenvolk. We are destined to rule." So instead of living peaceably with his neighbors, he got his armies together and started a war—and lost it. Cast into Hell, his pride exacerbated by his defeat, he vowed vengeance. Should he fight by force or by guile? Should he re-arm, supplying his munitions factories out of the apparently inexhaustible resources of Hell? Or should he sneak over an unfortified frontier, attacking a powerful God first through his weaker allies?

It was the latter plan that Satan put into effect. In Book II he appears as a practical politician, ingenious and not too scrupulous. He presides over the Council in Pandemonium and leaves the proposals of policy to the Number 2 Nazi, Beelzebub. Then when his plan is adopted he takes credit for it and goes his way, partly as a hero and partly as a liar. He is not only Hitler and Goering but Goebbels and to a certain extent von Ribbentrop. He will tell any lie and make any promise that will win a friend. He hasn't yet perfected any system of propaganda, however. He simply lies instinctively as occasion arises; evil, however splendid in its origins, must always do its business with falsehood and fraud.

In Book IV Satan invades neutral territory. The two human creatures in Paradise are harmless; in fact, Satan would never have suffered from their existence if he had not hunted them out and asked for trouble. Clearly Adam and Eve are the prototypes of all the gentle peoples whom Hitler has accused of aggression and warmongering. Finding them, Satan hates them and envies them, for the simple reason that they are peacefully minding their own business and enjoying, to a lesser degree, the comforts that he would still possess himself if he hadn't started the first of all world wars. He had once been happier than they and had thrown away happiness for ambition and a vain war of conquest. Now he hates all the peaceful ancestors of the Belgians and Norwegians who milk their cows and mind their gardens—hates them and envies them. Satan's pride in Book I may be noble; not so his envy and hatred in Book IV. It is easy enough for him to explain the invasion of Eden as a matter of military necessity and unfortified frontiers. I have read that Hitler surveyed the ruins of Warsaw and said, "How wicked people were to force me to do this!"

Shelley discovered in Satan "the taints of ambition, envy, revenge, and a desire for personal aggrandizement." He thought Milton had erred in letting these faults creep into the character of his hero. On the contrary, the faults are an integral part of the characterization of a villain. Pride goes with cruelty and cruelty with lust, in a perfectly correct Freudian pattern, and after them come all the petty vices of covetousness, envy, fraud, and malice. It is only in Book I that Satan is heroic, with splendid speeches about the unconquerable will and courage never to submit or yield. From that point on Milton charts the degradation of Satan, step by step.

Evil, as Milton understood it, is not a static but an active thing, and it becomes progressively more villainous and less and less heroic. The process has its outward and visible signs. In Book I, to be sure, Satan is still splendid, not "less than Archangel ruined," with "the excess of glory obscured." As the books go on, the glory disappears; the face and form are distorted so that Uriel can recognize the tokens a sun's distance away. Satan sits at the ear of Eve "squat like a toad," and in Book X, when he returns to Hell to report his triumphs, he feels his legs intertwining and falls prone to the ground, hissing, a serpent. That is Milton's ultimate comment on Satan and evil.

Milton once spoke of writing a poem "doctrinal to a

nation." *Paradise Lost* was doctrinal to his nation and his century, not to ours. It analyzed the problem of evil for a generation to whom evil was omnipresent and of terrific importance. As I said before, we have lost that conviction. I am not exaggerating when I say that a lack of Milton's comprehension of evil was one of our most serious unpreparednesses in the years when war was coming closer, and this same lack, I believe, is going to tempt us into ways of unwisdom when we come to make terms of peace.

Speaking as a student of literature, I have found three main currents of thought that have robbed us of a working theory of evil. I will take them up in the chronological order in which they entered the English-American mind. The first I shall call the sentimental theory, or the theory of the beautiful soul. It is a theory that identifies virtue with emotion, with beautiful impulses, with spontaneous outpourings of feeling. We can find the doctrine in some of our wisest teachers and loftiest poets—Wordsworth, Shelley, and Emerson, to name only three. The phrase *beautiful soul* was originally German, *schöne Seele*, and comes from the teachings of Friedrich Schiller, who we all agree belongs in the category of good, and also liberty-loving, Germans. "The beautiful soul we call a state where the moral sentiment has taken possession of all the emotions to such a degree that it may unhesitatingly commit the guidance of life to instinct." Or as a Frenchman put it, "Be beautiful and then do at each moment whatever your heart may inspire you to do."

Being on the whole goodhearted and sentimental, we have a natural inclination toward this theory. We like Wordsworth's couplet about

> Glad Hearts! without reproach or blot
> Who do thy work, and know it not.

There is nothing wrong in liking the idea of spontaneous goodness. The trouble comes when we lay the emphasis on the spontaneousness and don't inquire too carefully about the goodness. This is the catch—that delight in emotion may completely paralyze the critical intelligence. "I feel beautiful; I am beautiful; whatever I do is beautiful." Yet in practice, the things that that person does may be very ugly. Nobody doubts that beautiful impulses are good in themselves, but we Americans are inclined to trust them too exclusively.

The late Irving Babbitt dedicated himself to a lifelong assault on this theory. He loved to collect instances of beautiful souls doing unbeautiful things. He loved to read out a passage in which Rousseau dilates on his "warmth of heart," his "keenness of sensibility," and "the melting feeling, the lively and sweet emotion" that he experiences at the sight of everything that is virtuous, generous, and lovely. Then Babbitt would roll his eyes at his audience (of which I was one) and read the concluding sentence of Rousseau's paragraph: "And so my third child was put into the foundling hospital."

A quotation that is even more pertinent at the present moment comes from Robespierre. This is from a speech made before the National Convention at the very height of the Reign of Terror. The tumbrils were rolling up to the guillotine with their loads of victims, and it seemed that there was no limit to the blood that might be shed. In the midst of the blood, and while demanding still more blood, Robespierre could dilate on the beauty of virtue! "That tender, irresistible, imperious passion, torment and delight of magnanimous hearts, that profound horror of tyranny, that compassionate zeal for the oppressed, that sacred love of one's country, that still more sacred and sublime love for humanity." He could talk of finding "a celestial voluptuousness in the calm of a pure conscience and the ravishing spectacle of public happiness."

As Americans we are not likely to be fooled by anything

so hifalutin, but as Americans we do let ourselves be fooled into trusting emotional and beautiful souls without looking to see whether there are any reigns of terror in the background. To take a trivial instance, we are likely to put our trust in people who are kind to animals. Not long ago the *New Republic* had a charming little sketch of the entire office and editorial staff in a dither over the domestic life of a nesting pigeon. The whole episode was very virtuous and delightful, and if I had been there I should have been hanging out the window with everybody else. The sketch ended with an inference; namely, that this was evidence of the happy state of life in America.

That, as Babbitt would have said, is a false and Rousseauistic conclusion. I understand that Hitler is very kind to squirrels. Kindness to animals and kindness to human beings may go together and they often do. On the other hand, the beautiful soul may be feeding the squirrels with one hand and robbing widows and orphans or wiping out Lidice with the other. We should learn to beware of our instinctive confidence in beautiful emotions. We must be on guard against a reformed enemy who comes to us in virtuous tears.

Another kind of thinking that has confused our vision of evil I shall call the romantic theory. It is this theory that has transformed Satan from villain to hero. It runs this way. Energy is admirable; wickedness is energetic. "The tigers of wrath are wiser than the horses of instruction," said Blake. "Better to live as a lion for a day than for a hundred years as a sheep," said Mussolini. Quietness is contemptible; goodness is quiet. Therefore it follows that evil is good and good is bad. Q.E.D.

As is usual in any romantic theory, we find the name of Byron conspicuous. The Byronic hero in his successive metamorphoses has filled—and also written—more books than tongue can tell. He is volcanic, extreme in all things, magnificent in sin. He is adored of women (or, conversely, he is misunderstood and betrayed by women and retires into lofty isolation and the pageant of his bleeding heart). With the help of modern psychology he has developed complexes and neuroses. At times, to be sure, he evinces a spasmodic and spectacular goodness, but this is a manifestation of his superb energy and must never, according to the theory, be confused with the goodness of good people.

Early in the nineteenth century this theory got tangled up with Napoleon and also, with far-reaching consequences, with German philosophy. Students of the history of philosophy point to the doctrines of Fichte. From this source come the Superman, the Master Race, Prussianism, and Hitler. Until there was an actual outbreak in war, we did not resent this kind of thing because the ideas were not very different from ones that we had been brought up on. Not that many of us were fooled by Hitler as a person. A bad egg if ever there was one. Yet there was something comic about him, and we are such a good-natured people that we find it hard to realize that funny things can be dangerous.

Furthermore, we saw that Hitler and his friends had energy, and we rather admired them for it. We didn't blame them for not wanting to be bullied. We were inclined to discount the stories of domestic terrorism. Even after the war began in Europe, we felt a certain respect for Prussian competence and efficiency. We were genuinely confused by the romantic theory of evil. The thing that woke us up was not the badness of the egg but the terrific consequences of the things that particular egg did. When the war is over, unless I miss my guess, we are likely to be again misled into the same confusion of values.

There is still a third modern theory of evil, and this I shall call the scientific theory. According to this there is no such thing as sin. Human beings are merely very complicated mechanisms, and they are what they are because of the regular operation of heredity and environment, economic law, vitamin deficiency, hypertrophy of the glands, or whatever else you happen to believe in. Hitler is a paranoiac, and the whole German nation is suffering from a secondary, or induced, paranoia. Exponents of this theory remind us that science doesn't judge; it only explains. You can't blame Hitler for being a paranoiac any more than you blame poison ivy for being poisonous. Some day science will tell us what to do about it, but what if that day doesn't come soon enough?

Here are three ways of looking at the evil in human nature—the sentimental, the romantic, and the scientific. Each one of them has qualities that commend it to the American temperament. Our goodheartedness makes us like the first; our energy and independence incline us to the second; everything that is scientific in our education and training prepares us for the third. The fact that they are often contradictory doesn't worry us. Whatever our characteristic American virtues are, logic isn't one of them. We share with the other English-speaking peoples a genius for living happily with contradictions, anomalies, and compromises. And where does it all get us?

Let me return momentarily to Milton. Far be it from me to say that he knew all the answers, but he knew some of them. He knew that ambition leads to cruelty and terror; he knew that the human race can be saved only by goodness, the goodness of God in man. He knew that the forces of Hell are real and are everywhere and always. He saw them in his imagination, surging and seething and boiling up onto this earth. Theologies, to be sure, are transitory, far more transitory than poetry. So far as *Paradise Lost* is purely theological, it may be obsolete, but as an analysis of good and evil, it teaches a lesson that we still need to learn. Over the theology of the poem towers Satan, incarnate evil, the arch fiend, the destroyer, and on his head sits Horror plumed.

I should like to finish this chapter with a noble peroration on the splendors of American goodness, secure in its native right and triumphant over evil in all its forms; but I shall be on much safer ground if I merely sum up what I have said already. Taking us by and large, we have a considerable faith in goodness and good people. That faith is probably greater than we realize, and in this respect we are lucky, because a faith in the goodness of men is the one thing that democracy cannot do without. Beyond that we are entangled in a lot of familiar notions about good and evil, accepting now one and now another, never following any of them to their logical conclusions. We can get through this war, I am sure, on our faith in ourselves and our native goodness. It is after the war that we are going to run into trouble. Shall we look at Germany as a nation of beautiful souls, temporarily misled in their emotions but presently to return to an idyllic existence of Beethoven, beer, and Grimm's fairy tales? Or as a Byronic hero-nation, magnificent in sin, romantic in its defiant energy, and then tragic in its defeat? Or as the victim of an unfortunate environment, needing merely a treatment in international economic therapy?

Or shall we really get down to the roots of good and evil and wrestle with our theories until we bring them into some kind of working conformity, not only with one another but with fact?

V — Courage

There is no sanctuary for brave men,
  Danger allures them as it were a sun;
What they have dared they will dare once again.
  And so continue till the day is done.

There is no satiation of brave deeds,
  One draws another as wit calls on wit.
Oh, what a soul it is that ever heeds
  The hour's necessity and springs to it!

There's no intimidation of great thought,
  Knowledge attracts it as the heavens the eye;
Though dangerous 'tis to learn, it will be taught,
  Pushing its question to the uttermost Why.

There is no sanctuary for brave men,
  Danger allures them as the moon the tide;
What they have dared they will dare once again
  Though they lose all else in the world beside.

A. G. HERBERTSON, *There Is No Sanctuary for Brave Men*

The magpies in Picardy
Are more than I can tell.
They flicker down the dusty roads
And cast a magic spell
On the men who march through Picardy
Through Picardy to hell.

(The blackbird flies with panic,
The swallow goes like light,
The finches move like ladies,

The owl floats by at night;
But the great and flashing magpie
He flies as artists might.)
. . . .

He told me that in Picardy,
An age ago or more,
While all his fathers still were eggs,
These dusty highways bore,
Brown, singing soldiers marching out
Through Picardy to war.

He said that still through chaos
Works on the ancient plan,
And two things have altered not
Since first the world began—
The beauty of the wild green earth
And the bravery of man.

T. P. CAMERON WILSON, *Magpies in Picardy*

Chant you loud of punishments,
Of the twisting of the heart's poor strings
Of the crash of the lightning's fierce revenge.

Then sing I of the supple-souled men
And the strong, strong gods
That shall meet in times hereafter
And the amaze of the gods
At the strength of the men.
—The strong, strong gods—
—And the supple-souled men—

STEPHEN CRANE, *Three Poems, II*

—Now that our danger rises like the sun
Chasing all thin confusing mists away,
How fine, how proud, our wings of courage sweep.

VICTORIA SACKVILLE-WEST, *Personal Valour*

Through the long time the story will be told;
Long centuries of praise on English lips,
Of courage godlike and of hearts of gold
Off Dunquerque beaches in the little ships.

JOHN MASEFIELD, *To the Seamen*

Alone, above Manila's bay,
A falcon on the cloudy height,
He hung, and saw the battered shore,
The stinging hornet-swarm, the tight
Encircling fleet, and answering roar
Of that proud rock, Corregidor.

One bird of God in that still air,
One call to heaven before he fell,
To strike one blow, and strike it true.
He drew his breath and made his prayer,
And said a long and last farewell
To all he loved and all he knew.

He saw the ship in her dark pride,
Haruna of the Setting Sun.
He turned his wings above the wave,
Struck like an angry hawk—and died.
And that great ship went down. No gun
Will ever speak from her deep grave.

God grant our deaths may be as brave.

ROBERT NATHAN, *Captain Colin P. Kelly, Jr.*

A YEAR ago I was asked to give a radio talk on the novels
of this war. Well I knew that the good Lord never meant
me to be a radio speaker, but it did seem the right sort of
thing for an English teacher to do in wartime. Certainly I
couldn't work much harm, and I might even insert an idea

63

or two into the mind of a belated isolationist. In any case, it gave me a chance to go through a number of interesting new books. I told the lending library what I wanted and settled down to a comfortable month's reading at three cents a day.

I started without any particular idea of what I was going to find. I am not a person who keeps up, as they say, and although I had read a few of the best-sellers, I really knew less than most people about the subject I had promised to talk about. As I read, my first feeling was that I was learning a lot about the war. I liked especially the books by soldiers and war correspondents who were putting on paper the things they had seen and been through. Foremost among these was James Aldridge's *Signed with Their Honour*, and I have discovered since that a great many other people have been as impressed as I was. Aldridge went to Athens as a war correspondent at the time of the German invasion of Greece. His hero is a flyer in the Royal Air Force, and the book is dedicated to a flight squadron commander, another of the characters in the book, who gets killed before the story is over. There are vivid descriptions of the maneuverings of fighter planes and fights in mid-air above the mountainous landscape of Greece. It all has the same kind of actuality as the books that are plain records of fact like W. L. White's *They Were Expendable*. After I had read two or three more books of that sort I began to hope that somebody might really listen in to the radio talk and jot down some of the titles that I mentioned; they were important, immediate, necessary.

The next thing that struck me was the tremendous difference between these books and the books on war that I had been reading for the last twenty years. Practically all the older novels were studies of neurotic people in a dull world. Practically all the new ones seemed full of excitement and courage and even heroism.

Both novelists and poets who were writing between the wars were inclined to distrust courage. That came partly as a reaction against the heroics of the first great war. Too many people had talked too much about "our brave boys." The brave boys had seen too much that they didn't want talked about, particularly by fat stay-at-homes. The brave boys had seen fear and knew that it didn't belong with tea-table chatter at benefit bridges. They had seen horrors and horror. They had known men whose nerves had gone to pieces, whose personalities were shattered. All right, they said, we won't talk about it.

For another thing, the novels of the last twenty years grew out of an era of debunking. The novelists of the twenties and thirties were almost unanimous in their condemnation of war, and most of us in our ignorance thought that they were right. We had no means of foreseeing the catastrophe that lay before us. But their ridicule spread out in all directions and included not only flag wavings and Armistice Day speeches but also any kind of faith in devotion or patriotism or courage. The real truth, they said, is that human beings are basically cowardly and selfish, and it is hypocrisy to pretend that they ever do anything except save their own hides. The debunkers went on to say that all the acts that appear to be noble are either false or silly; either the people were not brave at all or they were idiotically brave when they did not need to be. Some people may be fooled into nobility, but the nobler they seem, the surer it is that they are being bamboozled by some super hypocrite behind the scenes. The villain of the piece may be a politician, a banker, an armament maker, or a bishop, but he and the novelist both know that the nobleness is all a fake. Heroes die so that hypocrites can double their profits.

Taking them by and large, the novels of this war are a fairly complete denial of this theory. Sometimes the refutation is deliberate and explicit, as it is in William Bradford

Huie's *Mud on the Stars,* although this isn't exactly a war book, except in the sense that it shows how the war has made men readjust their ideas. Huie's hero, who must be pretty much Huie himself, lies awake in an army camp and thinks over his life and his impressions of the last dozen years. The novel begins and ends with a protest against the prevailing estimate of human nature. "We have come to doubt that men are noble," he says at the beginning of the book, "and unless they are noble, why should they pretend to the right of self-government?" He comes back to the same theme at the end. "We are standing at the end of an era of debunking. Some of the debunking was good, but we carried it too far. In our efforts to smash false façades, we smashed some of the solid old foundation." It is Huie's hope that this war is going to bring us back to a faith in nobility and courage.

I believe that the immediate future of the world has been laid on the doorstep of the individual American. . . . If the individual American proves equal to the occasion, our century will become one of the glittering centuries of human history. . . .
I believe we will win. I believe that in spite of all the mud that has been splashed across the stars, the sons of the men who fought at Bunker Hill know that the stars are still there.

That is the final paragraph in the novel.

And that is in general the message—no, I won't say message; rather the *evidence* of the books of this war. In particular, the quality of courage stands out as one of the omnipresent characteristics of human nature. These books have been written by men with their eyes on the object. They have been written by people who have seen the war —seen bombs falling on London, defiance and sabotage in Norway, motor torpedo boats in the Philippines, airplanes over the North Atlantic and the mountains of Greece and the sands of Africa. What they have to say is that human nature is something tremendous and even awesome. They say that the quality of courage is almost universal. They don't say it sentimentally. They don't say it romantically. They simply set it down as a matter of observation that men are brave. Even if the authors are writing in the tradition of the debunkers, when they get to the things that they have actually seen they tell about courage. The lower middle classes may not be much to look at, but they can stand up to an awful lot of bombing. Even the congenital cowards have queer comic streaks of courage. All the reports from eyewitnesses tell us that human beings under fire have an almost undreamed-of nobility of character and of act, and yet I think that our writers still fight shy of any extravagant eulogies.

Novelists and journalists seem to have had an easier time of it than the poets. They are less self-conscious and they write more objectively. They can put a piece of heroism down in black and white and let it speak for itself. They make a point of giving you realistic details and bits of incongruity to make you understand that they are just as sophisticated as you are and wouldn't dream of recounting such extravagant stories if they hadn't seen these things with their own eyes.

But what about poetry? What have the poets been saying about war and heroism? In the 1920's and 1930's, very little. If they touched on such things at all, it was generally in the same mood that we noticed in the novelists. War was evil, crass folly, and only evil and stupid things came with it. But poets for the most part were dealing with a totally different kind of material. The characteristic poetry of the last two decades barely touched the major problems of life and conduct or the experiences of ordinary men. It was introspective, ingenious, subtle, allusive, difficult, "metaphysical" in the literary sense of the word. Poets devoted a large part of their skill to the precise recording of esthetic experiences and psychological niceties such as lie outside the range of the common reader. Even more than the novelists, the poets distrusted middle-class America and all its ways and works. They refused to cater to the bourgeois fondness for romance and heroics. If they described such things at all, they deflated them and flattened them out into prose.

Middle-aged people who were young in 1914 are disappointed today because there aren't any romantic war poems to learn by heart. They remember Seeger's "I have a rendezvous with death" and are disappointed in Spender's "I have an appointment with a bullet." Seeger says that he to his pledged word is true; Spender says prosaically, "And I shall not be late." It seems as though the poets are making a deliberate effort not to yield to the excitement of war. They are willing to write about its folly and cruelty but not about its glory and romance.

This resolve not to romanticize war and courage is certainly one of the characteristics of the poetry of these later years, but it doesn't mean that courage has disappeared from poetry. Here is a poem by Edwin Rolfe, written in the Spanish Civil War, that shows very well, I think, the desire to describe courage without heroics.

> Needless to catalogue heroes. No man,
> weighted with rifle, digging with nails in earth,
> quickens at the name. Hero's a word for
> peacetime. Battle
> knows only three realities: enemy, rifle, life.
>
> No man knows war or its meaning who has not
> stumbled from tree to tree, desperate for cover,
> or dug his face deep in earth, felt the ground pulse with
> the ear-breaking fall of bombs. No man knows war
> who never has crouched in his foxhole, hearing
> the bullets an inch from his head, nor the zoom of
> planes like a ferris wheel strafing the trenches. . . .
>
> War is your comrade struck dead beside you,
> his shared cigaret still alive in your lips.

68

"Hero's a word for peacetime," but the heroism is certainly there, no matter what you choose to call it.

If we leave the literature of the present moment and look back over our literature as a whole, no one can deny that we have a splendid panorama of brave men behind us. One always expects the earliest literature of a country to be full of stories of courage. The hero of the Old English epic killed the monstrous giant Grendel and then the monster's mother, and died at a ripe old age killing a dragon. Heroes of all the Germanic and Scandinavian poems were fighting the same kind of fights. In fact, Beowulf must have been a hero on the Continent before his people came to England.

The Beowulf manuscript was lost to sight long before Chaucer's day, and the story did not reappear until the nineteenth century. I put it in merely as one of the earliest documents of courage in the English tongue, for the literature of the Middle Ages produced the first set of literary ideas that have developed consecutively up to our time. In those days there was no literary barrier between the countries of western Europe. Arthur and his knights, Charlemagne and his paladins, Alexander the Great, the heroes of Troy and Thebes and the heroes of the Crusades, all moved freely together in the heroic pageant. It is recorded that William the Conqueror's minstrel went into the Battle of Hastings singing the Song of Roland, and the story of Roland's heroic death at Roncesvalles has been at home on English soil ever since. When Masefield told the story of Gallipoli in 1916, he took his chapter headings from the Song of Roland.

Oliver said, . . . "I have seen the Saracens: the valley and the mountains are covered with them; and the lowlands and all the plains; great are the hosts of that strange people; we have here a very little company."

Roland answered, . . . "My heart is the bigger for that. Please God and His holiest angels, France shall never lose her name through me."

Masefield might well have put beside it lines from one of the earliest English poems, "The Battle of Maldon."

> Up spake Byrhtwold, brandished his ash-spear,
> —He was a tried and true old hero,—
> Lifted his shield and loudly called to them:
> "Heart must be keener, courage the hardier,
> Bolder our mood as our band diminisheth."

The Renaissance carried on the international tradition. The men of Shakespeare's age read the great epics of Greece and Rome, Plutarch's Lives, the epics of modern Italy, and the history of their own heroic past all in the same spirit. These men believed that one read books in order to know how to live. One read about noble men in order to learn to be noble. One read about wicked men in order to learn to avoid their vices. In particular, one read about men of mixed vice and virtue in order to understand how even the noblest life can fail because of some tragic flaw. All great stories were full of what was called edification for one who was eager to learn. Moreover, if the reader identified himself with the hero, he was supposed somehow to become a better man in the process. He read about courage and felt stronger when he faced the next crisis. That is an old, old theory of the usefulness of books. It might be called the classical theory.

In contrast, one modern theory, the so-called theory of escape, assumes that we read noble stories merely to escape from our own ignoble lives. We forget ourselves, escape from boredom temporarily, and then return to our previous dullness untouched, unaltered by the new experiences. Dull women with dull husbands read about beautiful heroines adored by marvelous lovers; tired businessmen read about cowboys. Cowards read about heroes. According to the classical theory we read about beauty and courage and adventure because these things *are*. According to the escape theory we read about them because they *aren't*. We escape into a nonexistent world where things are heroic and then return to a totally disconnected world of dullness and meanness. If anything, we satisfy our feeble desire for virtue vicariously, and return to the real world even more reconciled than we were before to a life of contemptible nothingness.

Perhaps our choice of either of these two theories is a matter of temperament and varies from reader to reader. Personally I incline to the older theory, although I am forced to recognize a certain amount of truth in the newer one. I think I observe in myself the kind of response that the older critics postulated. As Sidney—Spenser's friend—said in the *Defense of Poesie,* "I never heard the old song of Percy and Douglas, that I found not my heart moved more than with a trumpet." I feel that way about a great many things besides the "Ballad of Chevy Chase." I feel that way about Shakespeare's *Henry V* and Tennyson's "The Revenge" and White's *They Were Expendable* and John Masefield's account of the evacuation of Dunquerque in *The Nine Days' Wonder.* I even feel that way about John Buchan's *Greenmantle* and *The Thirty-Nine Steps.* I can't help believing that books and conduct have worked back and forth on each other to produce a tradition of courage. Brave men do brave things. Other men write them down. Other men read them. Then more brave things get done and written down in an endless cycle. "Would you hear of an old-time sea-fight?" asks Walt Whitman.

> Would you hear of an old-time sea-fight?
> Would you learn who won by the light of the
>   moon and stars?
> List to the yarn, as my grandmother's father
>   the sailor told it to me.

It was in this spirit that Shakespeare wrote his historical plays. Here he told of the old-time fights that were the glory of England, along with the civil wars that had been her bane. In *Henry V* he came to the great climax of the pageant of English history in the Battle of Agincourt, the last great battle of the Hundred Years' War. I wish that I could say that this was a righteous war (as indeed it seemed to Shakespeare), but that is quite out of the question. It did, however, demonstrate the courage of ordinary men, the sort of men who make up an American army today. I think historians are inclined to agree with Shakespeare that in the breakup of the feudal system the best armies flourished in the most democratic countries. As Thomas Fuller wrote in the seventeenth century,

> If a state run up all to noblemen and gentlemen, so that the husbandmen be only mere labourers or cottagers, which one calls but housed beggars, it may have good cavalry, but never good bands of foot. . . . Wherefore, to make good infantry, it requireth men bred, not in a servile or indigent fashion, but in some free and plentiful manner.

To Shakespeare, Agincourt was a victory of Englishmen of all classes fighting together against an arrogant aristocracy. However you explain it, it was one of the miracles of history. The English were outnumbered five to one, far from their base, "hungry, weary, sore travelled," we read in Holinshed, "and vexed with many cold diseases." On the morning of the battle the Earl of Westmoreland looked about him at the pitiful army and wished they had "but one ten thousand of those men in England that do no work today." Not so, said the King.

> No, my fair cousin.
> If we are marked to die, we are enow
> To do our country loss; and if to live,
> The fewer men, the greater share of honour.

Henry's speech was recorded by the chroniclers, and it was already fine in the prose from which Shakespeare made his blank verse.

72

O, do not wish one more!
Rather proclaim it, Westmoreland, through my host,
That he which hath no stomach to this fight,
Let him depart; his passport shall be made,
And crowns for convoy put into his purse.
We would not die in that man's company
That fears his fellowship to die with us.
This day is called the Feast of Crispian.
He that outlives this day, and comes safe home,
Will stand a-tiptoe when this day is named
And rouse him at the name of Crispian.
. . . .

This story shall the good man teach his son;
And Crispin Crispian shall ne'er go by,
From this day to the ending of the world,
But we in it shall be remembered—
We few, we happy few, we band of brothers;
For he to-day that sheds his blood with me
Shall be my brother. Be he ne'er so vile,
This day shall gentle his condition:
And gentlemen in England now abed
Shall think themselves accursed they were not here,
And hold their manhoods cheap whiles any speaks
That fought with us upon Saint Crispin's day.

That kind of courage in the face of overwhelming odds
has been particularly dear to the English and American
mind. The essential thing has always been (as it was for
Emerson) the steadfast courage, not the outcome in victory
or defeat.

Though love repine and reason chafe,
There came a voice without reply,—
" 'Tis man's perdition to be safe,
When for the truth he ought to die."

I wonder if this feeling is particularly strong in the Bible-
reading countries, and especially in countries that read much
in the Old Testament. The Hebrews themselves were only
a handful of tribes in comparison with the great empires of
Assyria, Babylon, and Persia to the east and Egypt to the

south, but they were strong because they were on the Lord's side. The Lord smote the hosts of Pharaoh, the horse and the rider he cast into the sea. The Old Testament is rich in stories of men weak in themselves but brave in their trust in the Lord. If He would save them, well and good. If not, they could die for their faith. The martyrs of Reformation days heard their own voices in the words in which Shadrach, Meshach, and Abed-nego defied the great King Nebuchadnezzar.

Nebuchadnezzar . . . said unto them, Is it true, O Shadrach, Meshach, and Abed-nego, do not ye serve my gods, nor worship the golden image which I have set up?

Now if ye be ready that at what time ye hear the sound of the cornet, flute, harp, sackbut, psaltery, and dulcimer, and all kinds of musick, ye fall down and worship the image which I have made; well: but if ye worship not, ye shall be cast the same hour into the midst of a burning fiery furnace; and who is that God that shall deliver you out of my hands?

Shadrach, Meshach, and Abed-nego answered and said to the king, O Nebuchadnezzar, we are not careful to answer thee in this matter.

If it be so, our God whom we serve is able to deliver us from the burning fiery furnace; and he will deliver us out of thine hand, O king.

But if not, be it known unto thee, O king, that we will not serve thy gods, nor worship the golden image which thou hast set up.

Certainly our literature has taken its stories of heroism from all sources, but one of the greatest sources has been actual history. Read Tennyson's poem, "The Revenge," the tale of an English ship that fought a whole Spanish fleet off the Azores in the year 1591. As Froissart said of an earlier fight,

The battles on sea are more dangerous and fiercer than the battles by land: for on the sea there is no reculing nor fleeing; there is no remedy but to fight and to abide fortune, and every man to show his prowess.

Sir Walter Raleigh wrote "A Report of the Truth of the Fight about the Isles of Azores This Last Summer." Four years later a poet told how the captain, Sir Richard Grenville, was warned of the approach of the armada, but "staying to recover his men which were upon the Island, and disdaining to fly from his country's enemy, not being able to recover the wind, was instantly environed with that huge Navy, between whom began a dreadful fight, continuing the space of fifteen hours." Tennyson took the narratives as he found them in various places and turned them into a ballad, "The Revenge."

And the sun went down and the stars came out far over the
    summer sea,
But never a moment ceased the fight of the one and the fifty-
    three.
Ship after ship, the whole night long, their high-built galleons
    came,
Ship after ship, the whole night long, with her battle-thunder
    and flame;
Ship after ship, the whole night long, drew back with her dead
    and her shame.
For some were sunk and many were shattered, and so could
    fight us no more—
God of battles, was ever a battle like this in the world before?

There were battles like that in the last war; still more in this; still more to come. John Masefield's book on the ill-starred Gallipoli campaign is one of the great narratives of the same kind of courage.

The beach was heaped with wounded, placed as close under the cliff as might be, in such yard or so of dead ground as the cliffs gave. The doctors worked among them and shells fell among them and doctors and wounded were blown to pieces, and the survivors sang their song of "Australia will be there," and cheered the newcomers still landing on the beach. Sometimes our fire seemed to cease and then the Turk shells filled the night with their scream and blast and the pattering of their fragments. With all the fury and the crying of the shells, and the shouts and cries and cursing on the beach, the rattle of the small arms and the cheers and defiance up the hill, and the roar of the great guns far away, at sea, or in the olive groves, the night seemed in travail of a new age. All the blackness was shot with little spurts of fire, and streaks of fire, and malignant bursts of fire, and arcs and glows and crawling snakes of fire, and the moon rose, and looked down upon it all.

Masefield quotes a letter found on the body of a Turkish officer. (In that war the Turks were allies of Germany, and they were the victors in this campaign.) "These British are the finest fighters in the world. We have chosen the wrong friends."

We can still say with Sidney that our hearts are stirred "more than with a trumpet." The stories of the children in the fiery furnace, of Leonidas at Thermopylae, of Roland at Roncesvalles, of Agincourt, Gallipoli, and all the rest are woven together in our imaginations. In this war we have been most deeply moved, I think, by stories of the same sort, by the heroism of the small, stubborn armies of Norway and Greece, by the evacuation of Dunquerque and the beleaguered garrison of Corregidor, by the desperate stand at Stalingrad. True, it is often said that God is on the side of the big battalions, and doubtless we shall win this war partly because, given time, we can provide those battalions. Yet it is far more true that we shall win because we were born into a tradition of courage and faith. Let me quote from one more poem, Laurence Whistler's "In Time of Suspense."

> Another generation learns to die
> Gravely, not caring if the flags are flown,
> Believing simply it must save for Earth
> A way of life becoming to mankind,
> A grace of centuries, a thing of worth:
> This we believe, who by a peaceful hearth
> Have laughing eyes to-night, but are not blind.

VI   Sons of Martha

They do not preach that their God will rouse them a little
    before the nuts work loose.
They do not teach that His Pity allows them to leave their
    job when they damn-well choose.
As in the thronged and the lighted ways, so in the dark and
    the desert they stand,
Wary and watchful all their days that their brethren's days
    may be long in the land.

Raise ye the stone or cleave the wood to make a path more
    fair or flat;
Lo, it is black already with blood some Son of Martha
    spilled for that!
Not as a ladder from earth to Heaven, not as a witness to
    any creed,
But simple service simply given to his own kind in their
    common need.

RUDYARD KIPLING, *The Sons of Martha*

Whatsoever thy hand findeth to do, do it with thy might.

ECCLESIASTES

[John Bull] A terrible worker; irresistible against marches,
mountains, impediments, disorder, incivilization; everywhere
vanquishing disorder, leaving it behind him as method and
order.

THOMAS CARLYLE, *Past and Present*

The word of the Lord by night
To the watching Pilgrims came,
As they sat by the seaside,
And filled their hearts with flame.

God said, I am tired of kings,
I suffer them no more;
Up to my ear the morning brings
The outrage of the poor.

. . . .

I will have never a noble,
No lineage counted great;
Fishers and choppers and ploughmen
Shall constitute a state.

Go, cut down trees in the forest
And trim the straightest boughs;
Cut down trees in the forest
And build me a wooden house.

Call the people together,
The young men and the sires,
The digger in the harvest-field,
Hireling and him that hires;

And here in a pine state-house
They shall choose men to rule
In every needful faculty,
In church and state and school.

RALPH WALDO EMERSON, *Boston Hymn*

Many hamlets sought I then,
Many farms of mountain men . . .
Sweat and season are their arts,
Their talismans are ploughs and carts . . .

To fill the hollows, sink the hills,
Bridge gulfs, drain swamps, build dams and mills,
And fit the bleak and howling waste
For homes of virtue, sense and taste.

RALPH WALDO EMERSON, *Monadnoc*

I know a Jew fish crier down on Maxwell Street with a
    voice like a north wind blowing over corn stubble in
    January.
He dangles herring before prospective customers evincing
    a joy identical with that of Pavlowa dancing.
His face is that of a man terribly glad to be selling fish,
    terribly glad that God made fish, and customers to
    whom he may call his wares from a pushcart.

CARL SANDBURG, *Fish Crier*

THIRTY years ago Richard Cabot wrote a best-seller
called *What Men Live By*. I am told that it still sells.
According to Dr. Cabot, the things that we live by are
four: work, play, love, and worship. The one that he puts
first is work. He was a hard-working man himself and
thought that a good part of his happiness came from his
job. The happiest men among his friends were the hard
workers. As a doctor he was familiar with the neuroses
and invalidisms that go with idleness. He believed that if
you want to have the greatest number of healthy, cheerful
people in a democratic society, see to it that each one of
them has a job of work that he likes to do.

That is a normal American notion; I take it his readers
agreed with him. One reason why the book sells well is the
fact that it gives people a pleasant sense of self-approval.
"Right!" they say to themselves. "Look at me! *I* have al-

79

ways worked hard, and that is why I'm such a fine person!" Then they get up the next morning and go off to work with Dr. Cabot's blessing on their heads.

In 1940 when Marshal Pétain established a new government to succeed the Third French Republic, he announced a new formula for Frenchmen to live by: *Travail, famille, et patrie*. Work, family, and country were now to take the place of the liberty, equality, and fraternity of the three republics. I have no idea how the French populace responded to Pétain's pronouncement. Did they throw their caps in the air with joy, and cry with one voice, "Vive le Travail!" Work, the salvation of France? I doubt it. They were already working hard, too hard, and they resented being told that they had to work still harder.

Work, play, love, and worship. Work, family, and country. Work is work in any language, and the contrast is not between French and English or between Frenchman and American. The real difference, I think, lies in the liberty, equality, and fraternity that Pétain threw out of the window. Dr. Cabot was talking about the work of a free citizen in a democratic society; the fascist is thinking of the labor of human animals in a corporate state. Away with all this democratic hocus-pocus, says he. Enough of modernism and the rights of the individual and trade unions and forty-hour weeks! If you give people leisure to think in, they only make nuisances of themselves. Let the workingman work and then drag himself home too tired for anything except supper and bed.

I doubt if Dr. Cabot realized what a solid body of literature and tradition he had behind him, or how far back into the centuries his belief in work might take him. For the idea is there in the books as far back as Chaucer, the idea that work is a good thing and that a good man is a man who does his own job well. Go back once more to the Prologue and the twenty-nine pilgrims. Chaucer himself earned his living, though he doesn't tell us so, by collecting his majesty's customs and repairing the dikes at Greenwich. The knight's business was fighting and he was a good fighter.

> Ful worthy was he in his lordes werre
> And therto hadde he riden, no man ferre,
> As wel in cristendom as in hethenesse,
> And evere honoured for his worthynesse.

I know that according to Veblen's theory of a leisure class this was not work but an aristocratic form of leisure, but I cannot see that either Chaucer or the knight himself looked at it that way. The knight was a good knight and the yeoman was a good yeoman, and that was that.

The merchant was good at his bargains. The clerk—the student—studied indefatigably. The lawyer had all the law at his finger tips. The sailor knew everything there was to know about boats and harbors. The cook could roast and boil and broil and fry and make stews and pies (probably not the American kind but nonetheless good ones). The parson was the hardest working man of the lot. In sickness or distress, among rich or poor, no matter how long the journey or how bad the weather, he trudged out faithfully with whatever comfort he could offer.

> This noble ensample to his sheep he yaf,
> That first he wroghte, and afterward he taughte;
> Out of the gospel he tho wordes caughte.

If this is a good picture of fourteenth-century England—and we have every reason to suppose that it is—it was a country of busy, competent, self-reliant people. Even the cheats and chiselers labored hard at their skulduggery. If Chaucer pokes fun at them instead of raging at them as Langland did, it is partly because he admires the industry with which they pursued their unsavory callings. There is no suggestion that he prescribed one set of virtues for the aristocrats and another for the proletariat. Knight or plowman, it was all one. A country parson or a dirt farmer can read Chaucer's Prologue today and say to himself, "There were men like me in England six hundred years ago. Chaucer would have liked me!"

With Shakespeare and Spenser you enter a more romantic and much less American world. None of the interesting people work for a living. Antonio is a merchant, but his business seems to conduct itself off stage somehow, without any apparent supervision, and the one business transaction that is on record doesn't give us a very favorable impression of his acumen. The only person in *The Merchant of Venice* who keeps his mind on his knitting is the villain Shylock, and Shakespeare robs him of his daughter, his ducats, and his religion without a qualm. There were great merchants in Shakespeare's day, men like Sir Thomas Gresham, who founded the Royal Exchange and lent Queen Elizabeth money, but you can read a lot of Elizabethan literature without meeting them or gaining any notion of the importance they had in the England of their day.

Before Shakespeare died, however, there were ideas abroad in the land that were to lay a solid foundation for the American doctrine of work. The late sixteenth century saw the rise of the Puritanism that produced the New England colonies. When we use the word Puritanism today we are generally thinking of its moral implications, very often with a sense of disapproval. I am talking about Puritanism simply as a historical phenomenon. As the Church of England departed from the Catholic Church, so the Puritans went still farther in the same direction. They were the left-wingers and radicals of their day. Their importance was religious, political, economic, and social as much as it was moral. They gave us the English Sunday, to be sure, but also the Petition of Right and the Bill of Rights.

In the 1580's Sir Walter Mildmay, one of Queen Elizabeth's councilors, founded a new college at Cambridge.

"So, Sir Walter," said Elizabeth, "you have erected a Puritain foundation?"

"No, madam," said Mildmay. "Far be it from me to countenance anything contrary to your established laws; but I have set an acorn which, when it becomes an oak, God alone knows what will be the fruit thereof." The acorns of the acorns of that oak are still sprouting.

An English economist, R. H. Tawney, has an interesting book on the connections between Puritanism and business. The book is called *Puritanism and the Rise of Capitalism*, and its main theme is exactly what the title suggests. There are plenty of points in the argument that I could quarrel with, but there is a fundamental truth in the historical picture. The Puritan believed that God approved of work. The Puritan worked. He prospered. He believed that his prosperity was a sign of the Lord's approval. So he kept on working and prospering and praising the Lord.

There was nothing hypocritical about this. That is to say, there was nothing peculiarly or Puritanically hypocritical about it. (Wherever there are human beings there will be deliberate hypocrisy and also the kind of unconscious hypocrisy that we call rationalizing.) The Puritan was a great Bible reader, and when he read his Bible he read the Old Testament and the Epistles more than the four Gospels. In the Psalms he read that the righteous man shall be like a tree planted by the rivers of water.

His leaf also shall not wither; and whatsoever he doeth shall prosper. *The ungodly are not so.*

Seest thou a man diligent in his business? [says Solomon.] He shall stand before kings.

So Jehovah blessed the latter end of Job more than his beginning: and he had fourteen thousand sheep, and six thousand camels, and a thousand yoke of oxen, and a thousand she-asses.
He had also seven sons and three daughters.

Tawney quotes an early translation of Genesis: "And the Lord was with Joseph, and he was a lucky fellow." Truly, as Bacon says, prosperity is the blessing of the Old Testament.

It was in the seventeenth century that Englishmen and Americans were closest together in all sorts of ways. In spite of the three months' voyage, men, books, and ideas went back and forth across the Atlantic. In England the Puritan was diligent in his business and prospered, while the Cavalier wasted his substance on wine, cards, women, and an ungrateful king, and landed in a debtors' prison. In America the Lord's approval was even more obvious. It was only by hard work that the colonist cut down his trees and built his stockades, cleared his farms and reaped crops from a stony soil, caught his fish and salted them, and kept the stream of commerce flowing between the Old World and the New. "Not slothful in business," said the Apostle Paul, whom the Puritan refused to call Saint Paul; "fervent in spirit; serving the Lord."

The New World was the world for work. It is pleasant to serve God and prosper at the same time. If you want to leave God out of the picture, it is pleasant to do right and prosper at the same time. Thanks to a variety of causes, geography not being the least, it has been easy to combine these pleasures in this country—easier than almost anywhere else in the world.

> Bulkeley, Hunt, Willard, Hosmer, Meriam, Flint,
> Possessed the land which rendered to their toil
> Hay, corn, roots, hemp, flax, apples, wool and wood.
> Each of these landlords walked amidst his farm,
> Saying, " 'Tis mine, my children's and my name's.
> How sweet the west wind sounds in my own trees!"

The lines that I have just quoted come from Emerson. They suggest, I think, one of the important facts about the make-up of American society. Among us, from the beginning, hard work is to be found in combination with a great variety of other things—ownership of land, education, culture, independence of mind, and political and social importance. Free schools, town meetings, democratic church governments, and all the different social institutions that have grown up in new communities as circumstances demanded, have produced a kind of American personality that is almost unknown in older countries. It is hard for a European to realize that a man who looks sweaty and dirty and speaks with an odd accent may own a thousand acres and have intelligent and constructive ideas on agriculture. Thoreau was a philosopher and poet but also a kind of hired man and very handy with tools. Lincoln's rail-splitting is part of the tradition. Any politician who has been brought up on a farm or has worked his way through college will get a certain number of votes on that ground alone. In all sorts of ways, serious and absurd, American conduct is actuated by our belief in the importance of work.

I am not competent to give any kind of complete account of the development of notions of work. I only know that ideas of the sort keep cropping up in American literature. I could find plenty of quotations in Emerson, Thoreau, Alcott, and the rest of the nineteenth-century New Englanders, match them in Walt Whitman, and cap them with Vachel Lindsay, Carl Sandburg, and Robert Frost.

> The wind in the corn leaves among the naked stalks
> and the assurances of the October cornhuskers
> throwing the yellow and gold ears into wagons
> and the weatherworn boards of the oblong corncribs
> and the heavy boots of the winter roaring
> around the barn doors
> and the cows drowsing in peace at the feed-boxes—
> while the sheet steel is riveted into ships and bridges
> and the hangar night shift meets the air mail
> and the steam shovels scoop gravel by the ton
> and the interstate trucks parade on the hard roads. . . .

The people of Sandburg's *The People, Yes* are people laughing, talking, singing, dreaming, and above all working.

Perhaps what I have been saying sounds too simple and idealistic. I have been talking about work, work as one of the things that men live by, work as an article of American faith. I have said nothing about Labor with a capital L, or unemployment, or strikes. Moreover, I have ignored several obvious distinctions and talked as though the same generalizations would apply to merchants, surgeons, and ditch diggers.

As far as the distinctions go—between business and the professions, for instance, or between manual labor and mental—I make no apologies. I feel that they are generally either arbitrary or irrelevant. The real distinction is between people who work as individuals and people who work by the hundreds. The first group I know quite a lot about, and for them I think all the things I have been saying remain substantially true. One chapter in *What Men Live By* is "The Points of a Good Job," and one of the most important points is this: "A chance to achieve, to build something and to recognize what we have done." I should add to that, "A chance to feel that we are doing something *well*."

It is all plain sailing when we are talking about people like Dr. Cabot himself. I remember that when I was a child my father, who was a normal-school teacher, was offered a principalship. My mother felt she ought to explain to us why he didn't take it. "You might like us to have more money," she said, "and you might think it was nice to be the principal's children. But your father would hate it. What he wants to do is teach. He *loves* to *teach*."

My observation tells me that the same kind of pleasure attaches to all sorts of jobs, even jobs that seem to me personally trivial, disagreeable, or dull. (People who don't like teaching think teaching is dull.) In my experience practically anybody who is good at his job is pleased with himself We all know how a man settles into his chair with a little circle of listeners and starts out, "Now in my business . . ." We all know the smile of the garage mechanic who emerges from under the car with the trouble spotted. He *knows* and he *can do*. I often think of a cleaning woman who worked for me for many years. She pitied me because I had to read so much instead of doing interesting things with soap and water. When she said she helped me, she meant it. She thought of herself as constantly rescuing me from a series of domestic catastrophes. "If Miss Jackson could only use her head like I do," she would say to her other ladies. "But no, she is always at that school."

It is when I turn to the people who work by the hundreds and thousands that I get into trouble; when I leave work and start on labor. It is then that I run into argument, prejudice, bitterness, hate, and fear; conflicting theories; misunderstandings and misrepresentations; contradictory statements even about what ought to be ascertainable facts. I am not naïve enough to think I can solve the problems of the CIO with Chaucer and Emerson. Only the workingman himself knows all the things that are wrong in the working world.

We have made a special American conjugation for the verb *to work*.

> I work
> You work
> He, she, and they *ought* to work

Then we take ideas about our own good jobs and carry them over, unmodified, to other people's bad jobs. In a society like ours there are thousands of bad jobs, jobs that Dr. Cabot couldn't turn into good ones by any kind of point system. When a coal miner comes up from a long day underground, you can't greet him with lines from Robert Frost.

The fact is the sweetest dream that labor knows.

87

> "Men work together," I told him from the heart,
> "Whether they work together or apart."

I know what I would say to poetry like that if I were a coal miner.

Even so, I am not ready to give up my chapter on the American idea of work. It is an American characteristic to be able to find ways out of a jam. Indeed it would be American to figure out a system of checks and balances and compensations for bad jobs—millions of bad jobs. It would be work to figure out such a system. It would mean applying to people the same kind of thinking that we devote to problems in mechanics. It would be American to do just that thing. We could study the resiliency of human nature as carefully as we study the resiliency of steel. We know about the right temperatures for machines. There are right emotional temperatures for people, neither subzero nor boiling point. It would be American to find out these things. It would be American to put this kind of technical information to practical use.

Heaven help us, don't think that I am about to solve the labor problem! I merely stand by the main thesis of this book. Americans have the capacity to work out solutions for this problem as well as for so many others. When the answer comes it will come practically rather than theoretically, but still within the framework of the traditional, democratic theory of work, Dr. Cabot's and not Marshal Pétain's. It may even owe something to Emerson. Writing an essay on the American scholar, Emerson turns from the scholar's character and training to his duties, the duties of Man Thinking. When we come to an American solution of the labor problem it won't be in terms of workmen or laboring classes. It will deal with people, *people working*.

VII The New Atlantis

Here first the duties of to-day, the lessons of the concrete,
Wealth, order, travel, shelter, products, plenty;
As of the building of some varied, vast, perpetual edifice,
Whence to arise inevitable in time, the towering roofs, the
    lamps,
The solid-planted spires tall shooting to the stars.
      WALT WHITMAN, *The United States to Old World Critics*

Lay me on an anvil, O God.
Beat me and hammer me into a steel spike.
Drive me into the girders that hold a skyscraper together.
Take red-hot rivets and fasten me into the central girders.
Let me be the great nail holding a skyscraper through blue
    nights into white stars.
      CARL SANDBURG, *Prayers of Steel*

Out of John Brown's strong sinews the tall skyscrapers
    grow,
Out of his heart the chanting buildings rise,
Rivet and girder, motor and dynamo,
Pillar of smoke by day and fire by night,
The steel-faced cities reaching at the skies,
The whole enormous and rotating cage
Hung with hard jewels of electric light,
Smoky with sorrow, black with a splendor, dyed
Whiter than damask for a crystal bride
With metal suns, the engine-handed Age.
      STEPHEN VINCENT BENET, *John Brown's Body*

An American Credo

For the king had at sea a navy of Tarshish with the navy of Hiram: once every three years came the navy of Tarshish, bringing gold, and silver, ivory, and apes, and peacocks.

So king Solomon exceeded all the kings of the earth in riches and in wisdom.

I KINGS

> Gold and iron are good
> To buy iron and gold;
> All earth's fleece and food
> For their like are sold.

EMERSON, Politics

Galileo, Galileo, come up from the tomb; you are going
    to War
Listen
On the railroad yards of all the men who kick out the col-
    lege professors, the 100-lb. bomb and the 4,000-lb.
    bomb strike as you said, simultaneously

In landing barges that slip onto the beaches where the debt-
    ridden, brute-ridden peasant looks out to sea, the com-
    mandos synchronize their watches with your pendulum

Toward the harbors of cities where the great books are
    burnt in the public squares, the battleships navigate,
    as you directed, by the stars

Centering the crosshairs on a man who made the scholars
    feed on the slop of darker ages, the sniper aims his rifle
    with a telescopic sight—your lenses in a hollow tube

Whistling into the last pillboxes of the tough guys who
    fondle the old men with rubber hoses, the artillery
    shells fall, as you calculated, in the true Galilean
    parabola

And if you wish, Galileo, the infantry will charge the final
objective shouting your whisper, "It moves, for all
that!" knowing that what it moves around is now and
always—high, clean, bright—the Sun

PRESTON NEWMAN, *Galileo Goes to War*

IN HIS old age, after the *Essays* and *The Advancement of
Learning* and the *Novum Organum* and all the rest, Bacon
began one last book, which he called *The New Atlantis*.
He left it unfinished, and it was published in 1626 after his
death. It starts out like a story of adventure, and you don't
know at first that you aren't reading Jules Verne or *Gulliver's Travels*. "We sailed from Peru, where we had continued by the space of one whole year, for China and Japan,
by the South Sea." Driven off their course in the South
Pacific the mariners come to a previously undiscovered
island and enter into a good haven, the port of a fair city,
"not great indeed, but well built, and that gave a pleasant
view from the sea."

The island is called Bensalem, obviously reminiscent of
the Biblical Salem for which so many towns have been
named. The people, though utterly unknown to Europeans,
are Christians and have reached an incredibly high state of
civilization. Astonishingly enough, they seem to be completely informed about conditions in Europe, its political
institutions, culture, science, inventions, and so forth, and
they have adopted everything European that is good and
discarded everything that is bad. In fact, the island is obviously governed by superlatively wise and unselfish men.

By this time it is clear that the story is not only that of
an imaginary voyage but an account of an ideal republic.
The most remarkable thing in Bensalem is a foundation, or
order, or society called Solomon's House. "The noblest

foundation, as we think, that ever was upon the earth, and the lantern of this kingdom. It is dedicated to the study of the works and creatures of God." Its object is this: "the knowledge of causes, and secret motions of things; and the enlarging of the bounds of human empire, to the effecting of all things possible." Put into modern English, that means the study of science for the purpose of controlling nature and producing the greatest possible degree of physical well-being for mankind. Bacon had explained in some of his earlier books that science had accomplished little up to this time because it lacked the proper procedure for research, but now that the new method had been expounded by Bacon himself he saw no limit to the discoveries and inventions of the future.

Supplied by the state with apparently unlimited funds, Solomon's House had laboratories and equipment for every possible kind of scientific research, with corresponding facilities for recording and correlating discoveries. There was a complete program for agricultural biology, botany, and chemistry, with investigations into soils and fertilizers. The experts increased the size of fruit and vegetables, produced them out of season, and invented new kinds, combining various desirable qualities. (All this in 1626!) The doctors had new medicines and new treatments for disease —by heat and cold, for instance. A refrigerating system had been invented, and it is a matter of record that Bacon himself died from a cold that he caught experimenting with the preservative powers of snow. There were new methods of producing light and methods of transmitting light and sound over great distances. The meteorologists had not only studied weather but had made some progress in producing the kinds of weather desired. There were new kinds of "papers, linen, silks, tissues," with excellent dyes. There were boats that went under water, and also "some degrees of flying in the air." There were also vast improvements in artillery and explosives, for the wise men of Solomon's House felt that even an undiscovered island should be ready to protect itself against invasion.

To put the thing in a nutshell, the scientists of Bensalem had examined the discomforts and disabilities of mankind and proceeded to remove them by scientific means, and they had also examined the natural, wholesome desires of men and proceeded to gratify them. As I say, the book was still unfinished when Bacon died, six years after the founding of Plymouth, less than twenty after the founding of Jamestown. It is a very American book.

By way of footnote, let me turn to a speech by Thomas Henry Huxley, delivered in 1866 and published in 1870, "On the Advisableness of Improving Natural Knowledge." Huxley begins his lecture with an account of the two violent catastrophes of seventeenth-century London, the Great Plague of 1665 and the Great Fire of 1666. The former, he says, was accepted as a judgment of God; the latter was resented as the work of some malicious human agency, either Catholic or Puritan according to your politics. Huxley goes on to show that there has been no recurrence of either kind of catastrophe, not because of any change in human nature or in the ways of God but simply because of the advances of science. The invention of the force pump has made it possible to put out fires. Increased knowledge of hygiene, sanitation, and prophylaxis has made it possible to prevent plague. Huxley points out also that an increased facility with mathematics has permitted insurance companies to mitigate the effects of the lesser catastrophes that still occur.

The moral of all this, in Huxley's mind, is the value and "advisableness" of scientific research. An event much more important even than either the Great Plague or the Great Fire was the organization of the "Royal Society of London for Improving Natural Knowledge," which began with

93

the meeting of a small group of friends in 1645 and received a charter and an endowment in 1662. It is recorded that its founders got their inspiration from *The New Atlantis* and Solomon's House and thought of themselves as putting Bacon's ideas into practice. This was the beginning in England of the association of men of science for the furthering of their common object. There were famous scientists in the group: Sir Isaac Newton, the Boyle of Boyle's law of gases, the Halley of Halley's comet. There were men of letters as well and also men of high social position. Boyle was once described in all seriousness as "father of chemistry and brother of the Earl of Cork." They illustrated splendidly the theory that Housman expressed in one of his lectures that "there is no rivalry between the studies of Arts and Laws and Science but the rivalry of fellow soldiers in striving which can most victoriously achieve the common end of all, to set back the frontier of darkness."

The whole business is thoroughly American or thoroughly English, whichever you choose to say, because this is one of the ways in which we are more English than the English themselves. If I had been writing thirty years ago I might in my ignorance have said also thoroughly German, because it looked then as though Germans in Germany were carrying out Bacon's project as wholeheartedly as any of us. How the idea went wrong in Prussia is another story. In Western Europe in general and among the English-speaking peoples everywhere the idea remains substantially what it was in Bacon's fantasy—the advancement of science for the well-being of mankind, or, conversely, the progressive increase in human comfort and achievement as a result of the progress of science and invention. In the last twenty-five years we have watched the process by which Russia has deliberately and with tremendous concentration of effort added herself to the list of Baconian countries. And I keep coming across statements by distinguished Chi-

nese writers to the effect that this will be one of the chief
objectives of China when this war is over and the affairs of
peace once more have first place.

It is interesting that Bacon's ideal was first expounded in
the same years when England was making herself a New
World on this side of the Atlantic. There are close connections between scientific progress and American democracy.
As Guy Stanton Ford once pointed out, it is inventions like
rayon that have made the Colonel's lady and Judy O'Grady
sisters *over* the skin. I submit that a belief in the constant
improvability of human living is as essential a part of American faith as any other doctrine that you could name.

From this point on there are all sorts of directions in
which the mind may proceed. I should like to set down
more or less disconnectedly three or four ideas about the
modern manifestations of the spirit of *The New Atlantis*.

It strikes me first that Bacon's ideas coincide—I won't
argue about cause and effect—with the American fondness
for getting things done and also with the American notion
that it is right to get things done. We have a strong moral
streak in us, which is a constant irritation to one kind of
highbrow, and we like to feel that we are doing right. In
one course that I teach every year, we study Marlowe's
Doctor Faustus and Bacon's *New Atlantis* within a few
weeks of each other, and the two books make an interesting
contrast. Doctor Faustus was a very learned man who sold
his soul to the devil in order to get unlimited knowledge,
wealth, pleasure, and power. The story belongs to a large
body of literature about magic and witchcraft and utilizes
only a handful of ideas out of a much larger fund of information. The basic assumption is that the magician's desire
for increased knowledge, wealth, pleasure, and power was
hellish. Certain limits were ordained within which the good
man might enjoy himself virtuously and humbly. The desire
to overstep those bounds was diabolical. Moreover, the at-

tainment of desires outside these fixed limits necessitated the intervention of the devil himself.

It is interesting to see what a magician was supposed to be able to do. He could, for one thing, get himself transported with phenomenal speed, sometimes through the air. (One list of Elizabethan stage properties includes "One dragon for Faustus.") He could know about things that were happening at a distance. He could control the weather. He could produce flowers and fruits out of season. He could invent marvelous instruments of war. Altogether the magician did with the help of Satan just about the same things that Bacon contemplated accomplishing with the help of science. There is no question which point of view characterizes America today.

The change did not come all at once. There has been a perennial protest against interfering with the ways of God. The force pumps and fire departments that Huxley talks about once met opposition from men who objected to the impious procedure of putting out fires. If the Lord wanted a house to burn down, it was defying His will to pump water on the flames. In spite of which attitude, fire departments have flourished. The conflict wasn't really between science and religion, for in point of fact churchmen have often been staunch friends of scientific progress. Cotton Mather was a corresponding member of the Royal Society and, contrary to the popular impression, was one of the most ardent defenders of the new scientific discoveries, including inoculation for smallpox. The important contrast between *Doctor Faustus* and *The New Atlantis* is the contrast between two conceptions of what is right or, if you wish to speak religiously, between two interpretations of the will of God. According to Baconian-American twentieth-century theory, it is the will of God that men should use their God-given minds to enhance the comfort of themselves and their neighbors.

The spirit of Bacon speaks in a prayer that the Dean of Canterbury wrote a few years before the war for a modern group of Canterbury pilgrims.

Give us, we pray thee, skill to speed our ploughs,
To set our engines working,
To pursue the paths of science,
To quicken enterprise and stimulate invention,
And so to solve the problems of exchange and distribution
That we be no longer tempted to destroy, or to restrict,
    or to withhold the things men lack,
Nor to suffer needless want in a world where
Thy plenty abounds.

A second idea that comes to me is the connection between science and commerce. It is quite obvious that modern commerce has flourished largely because of improvements in transportation and communication and also inventions whereby products are preserved and made more transportable—all in the spirit of *The New Atlantis*. In the seventeenth and eighteenth centuries the desire for wealth and comfort obtained the blessing of the Lord. It was not necessary to sell one's soul to the devil. One was diligent in business (see Proverbs and also my preceding chapter) and wealth flowed into one's coffers.

It is interesting to see this idea appearing in literature as the merchant begins to take his place as one of the important figures of English life. One of the most popular plays of the eightenth century was *The London Merchant; or, The History of George Barnwell*. The merchant is significantly named Thorowgood, the wealthy and virtuous father of a beautiful daughter. He has two apprentices, one of whom, Trueman, follows in his master's footsteps, whereas the other, George Barnwell, is seduced from the paths of industry into unchastity, theft, and murder.

It is interesting to hear Thorowgood discourse upon commerce, which, he says, is founded on reason and the

nature of things. He points out "how it promotes humanity, as it has opened and yet keeps up an intercourse between nations far remote from one another in situation,
customs and religion; promoting arts, industry, peace and
plenty, by mutual benefits diffusing mutual love from pole
to pole."

The virtuous apprentice listens attentively and adds his
own contribution, obviously inspired by the convictions of
the author of the play. "I have observed those countries
whose trade is promoted and encouraged do not make discoveries to destroy, but to improve mankind by love and
friendship."

I have no desire to involve myself in a debate over
theories of capitalism; I merely want to point out some of
the literary antecedents of American points of view, and
I can't leave this particular topic without adding at least
one other quotation from the eighteenth century. This
comes out of a *Spectator* of 1711. It was written by Richard Steele, but it could easily be matched with passages
from Addison. It is from a description of one of Sir Roger
de Coverley's friends, "a merchant of great eminence in the
city of London."

> He is acquainted with commerce in all its parts, and will tell
> you that it is a stupid and barbarous way to extend dominion
> by arms: for true power is to be got by arts and industry.
> . . . I have heard him prove that diligence makes more lasting
> acquisitions than valor, and that sloth has ruined more nations
> than the sword. . . . He has made his fortune himself, and
> says that England may be richer than other kingdoms by as
> plain methods as he himself is richer than other men.

It is worth remembering that *The Spectator* was part of
every gentleman's library in the American colonies and that
Benjamin Franklin and his friends studied the volumes dili-
gently and learned from them a great many things besides
the niceties of English style.

For the third of my miscellaneous ideas, I will remark that *The New Atlantis* is the spiritual ancestor of what we call the machine age, and that the machine age has faults as well as virtues. I will add also my personal conviction that the critics of our age have frequently been too harsh in their condemnations and have tended to compare a well-known and realistic present with a vague and idealized past. For instance, it is often said that all modern America is standardized and vulgarized, and our population is contrasted unfavorably with the noble peasantry of other places and times—people ignorant of machines and commerce but wise in the ways of nature and the everlasting cycles of birth and procreation and death. It is easier to demonstrate the ignorance than the wisdom. I have strayed through parts of southern France where the course of life can hardly have changed very much since Caesar's Gallic Wars. Sometimes on a path in the hills I have come face to face with a peasant and a great white ox and contemplated the two faces. There was never any doubt which countenance was nobler, and it was an open question which showed more intelligence. I think the critics who deplore our standardization have neglected to consider the appalling standardization of stupidity.

Pessimists have bestowed a great deal of pity on the dismal victims of our mechanized life. I can't help thinking that most of the pity has been wasted. We *like* machines. One thing that stands out in those war novels I read last year is the delight that men take in their machines. "I felt good," says one hero, "so I stepped on the gas." The flyers like their airplanes, and the mechanics like their engines, and the gunners like their guns. The capacity for excitement resides in the individual himself rather than in any external object. If the machine age has done nothing else it has increased the possibilities of excitement and put them within reach of a larger part of mankind.

This is one of the essential qualities of his own age that Kipling realized and turned into poetry. In a list of the qualities that made Kipling popular André Maurois puts first his consciousness of the heroic view of life. It is just as significant, I believe, that Kipling ascribed heroism and romance to the modern world of machines. The commuters complained that romance was dead, and "all unseen, Romance brought up the nine-fifteen." "M'Andrew's Hymn," "The Miracles," "The Bridge-Builders," "The Destroyers," "The Liner She's a Lady"—the list would take a page. Any study of contemporary poetry brings out our growing realization of the excitement and beauty of the world of machines.

Another charge against our age has been that comfort and commerce have made us soft. That was part of Hitler's indictment of the democracies, and here is at least one critic who has had reason to change his mind. It is true enough that if you look in the right places you can find evidence that a mechanical civilization has reduced us to helplessness. I sometimes listen to a news broadcast sponsored by a bakery, and I shall never forget those weeks in which we were instructed daily in the difficult art of detaching a slice of bread from an unsliced loaf. In actual practice, though, we seem to be just about as active and energetic and competent as any of our ancestors. Our soldiers appear to compare favorably with soldiers of sturdy peasant stock. Civilization and comfort, good plumbing, good beds, and good food have made us big and healthy and tough. Adrift on a life raft we endure physical hardship and also exhibit a remarkable competence in snaring seagulls and killing sharks with jackknives. The evidence of these years seems to be that the American at war can do as good a job as the next man, with machines or without.

One last indictment of the machine age I must mention and must also submit to. Our modern Atlantis is incredibly

rich. Our investigation of scientific law has far outgrown
the imagination of any single individual. Our applications
of scientific law are a perennial marvel. But our comprehension of life? Our personal processes of scientific thinking?
Our wisdom? Are they so satisfactory to contemplate? I
was an undergraduate when the first transcontinental tele-
phone call was made, and I remember that the college
preacher gave us a sermon on the text, "What shall it profit
a man to talk from Boston to San Francisco if he has nothing to say?" The question is still pertinent.

Our World's Fairs give us noble object lessons on our
scientific progress—halls of science, halls of medicine, halls
of transportation, halls of agriculture. I used to watch the
crowds that trailed through the Century of Progress in
Chicago. A family would go through the Hall of Science
conscientiously and admiringly, upstairs, downstairs, and
out the other side. Then they would look at the sign on
the next booth and pay twenty-five cents apiece to have
their palms read. That is a kind of discrepancy for which
our New Atlantis has provided no adequate remedy.

I cannot do better than to quote from a lecture by John
T. Tate of the University of Minnesota. This was a Sigma
Xi lecture, and the first half of the talk traced the history of
our knowledge of electricity in a way that would have delighted the heart of Bacon. Then came these paragraphs:

The other evening a naval officer, himself a physicist, and I
were sitting together in my rooms. Although once closely
associated we had not seen each other for a number of years
and our conversation was perhaps more philosophical than normal, partly because we realized that in less than 24 hours we
would be 6,000 miles apart—he in Scotland and I in Los
Angeles.

We were listening to a short wave broadcast from Berlin.
The speaker by every trick of oratory and persuasion, by spe-
cious lies, by distortions of the truth, by appeal to racial prejudices and to religious differences was attempting to create

dissension and disunity in America. A moment later we heard an unctuous voice from one of our own broadcast studios extolling to a gullible public by the same tricks, though the distortion of truth was now kept within legal bounds, the virtues of some snake oil preparation, which he said science shows is 52 per cent more something or other than any other concoction.

As thinkers about nature we could appreciate the long and patient search for truth which made this projection of a human voice through space and over the Atlantic possible. But as men thinking about nature we were nauseated by these unworthy desecrations of a beautiful thing.

It is not that we have done wrong to follow the vision of the New Atlantis. Bacon's world is our world. Nothing is more surely a part of our make-up than the Baconian faith that man, with the help of science, can coerce the physical universe. More and better machines; more cars, airplanes, vacuum cleaners, telephones, automobiles, radios; more and more gadgets; and if we are forced into a war, the best of all possible guns and tanks and Flying Fortresses. That is the faith and the story of America. But not the whole faith or the whole story.

VIII   *Education*

Democracy alone among forms of government has everything to gain and nothing to lose from the intelligence of
its citizens.

C. E. M. JOAD, QUOTED IN *The Observer*

> Each honest man shall have his vote,
> Each child shall have his school.

RALPH WALDO EMERSON, *Boston*

He who first shortened the labor of Copyists by device of
Movable Types was disbanding hired Armies and cashier-
ing most Kings and Senates and creating a whole new Democratic world: he had invented the Art of printing.

THOMAS CARLYLE, *Life of Frederick the Great*

> Cannon-parliaments settle naught;
> Venice is Austria's,—whose is Thought?
> Minié is good, but, spite of change,
> Gutenberg's gun has the longest range.

JAMES RUSSELL LOWELL, *Villa Franca, 1859*

Here, then, is that freedom, or exercise of enlightened choice,
by which I define that which is variously called "humane,"
"humanity," "humanistic," "humanism," or "liberal culture."
Its specifications are: learning, imagination, sympathy, dig-

103

nity and civility. You may recognize them by their opposites. The man who lacks freedom is ignorant, narrow, indoctrinated or dogmatic, through lack of learning; literal-minded, pedantic, habituated or vulgar, through lack of imagination; insensible, apathetic, prejudiced, censorious, opportunistic, sordid or self-absorbed, through lack of sympathy; base, ascetic, trivial, or snobbish, through lack of dignity; dull, boorish, or brutal, through lack of civility.

RALPH BARTON PERRY, *The Meaning of the Humanities*

Meek young men grow up in libraries, believing it their duty to accept the views which Cicero, which Locke, which Bacon, have given; forgetful that Cicero, Locke, and Bacon were only young men in libraries when they wrote these books.

RALPH WALDO EMERSON, *The American Scholar*

Prove all things; hold fast that which is good.

I THESSALONIANS

And ye shall know the truth, and the truth shall make you free.

JOHN

Lords and Commons of England," said Milton, "consider what Nation it is whereof ye are. . . . A Nation not slow and dull, but of a quick, ingenious, and piercing spirit, acute to invent, subtle and sinewy to discourse, not beneath the reach of any point the highest that human capacity can soar to."

What Milton could say of England in 1644 we can say with equal truth of America three hundred years later. As a nation we are not slow and dull. We have quick, ingenious, and piercing minds; we are still acute to invent. Even if our best minds fall short of the highest point that human capacity can soar to, it would be hard to find other minds in other countries that are soaring much higher. Yet we are capable of all the inconsistencies with which I ended my last chapter. Such people as we are!

It is not that we have not tried to educate ourselves; still less that we do not *believe* in educating ourselves. In fact, I should put faith in education as one of the most steadfast articles in the American creed. We spend time; we spend money; we exhaust the devoted energy of thousands of teachers; and still ignorance and stupidity and folly walk our streets. And why? For the simple reason, I think, that educating human beings is the hardest task we can possibly set ourselves. I was instituting a false analogy when I contrasted the perfection of our machines with the imperfections of the uses to which we put them. Once the way is discovered, perfect machine follows perfect machine in infinite succession, but no scientist has yet discovered a way by which to produce even a second identical mind, let alone a two-hundredth or a two-thousandth. No one has invented an intellectual blast furnace that will smelt out stupidity!

Verily, education is the most difficult of all human endeavors—so difficult, indeed, that few nations have even attempted it. The education of a few gifted souls, as in Athens or Jerusalem or Peking is, comparatively speaking, an easy task, yet we have no record that the education of even the most gifted minds under the most favorable circumstances has ever been completely successful. Consider, then, the education of all the children of all the parents in all the states of this heterogeneous conglomeration of peoples that we call a nation! Is it faith or madness that makes us attempt it? And is not the very fact of the attempt one of the most astounding demonstrations of the vigor of American democracy?

It is interesting to inquire how early in our history this faith in education developed. The answer, as it does so frequently, takes us back across the Atlantic to England. Obviously, popular education could not have been even imagined until after the invention of printing and the establishment of Caxton's first English printing press in 1477. We find its root in the religious beliefs of that same body of Puritan Englishmen who gave us our faith in work. As I said in an earlier chapter, Queen Elizabeth and one great party in the Church of England would have been content with a purified and Anglicized Catholic church. They would have purged the church of the abuses that Catholicism itself denounced in the Counter Reformation; they would have simplified the services, centered authority in England instead of Rome, and then stopped. Not so the Puritans.

For the Puritan reformer the heart of Christianity was not in an institution or a potentate but in a Book. "All scripture is given by inspiration of God, and is profitable for doctrine, for reproof, for correction, for instruction in righteousness: that the man of God may be perfect, throughly [*i.e.*, thoroughly] furnished unto all good works." Everything necessary to salvation was to be found in the Bible. Any individual soul, not infant, idiot, or lunatic, was endowed with the capacity for discovering the will of God as set forth in his Word. But—and here begins the history of popular education—in order to discover the will of God in the sacred Book, every true Christian must be able to read.

The Middle Ages had developed the education of clergy, doctors, lawyers, and learned clerks. With the Renaissance came the education of gentlemen. The Reformation saw the disestablishment of monks and clergy and the rise of the trading classes and saw also the founding of grammar schools. Such was Stratford Grammar School, which taught Shakespeare a little Latin and less Greek. But it was only late in Shakespeare's century that Puritan teaching began to insist on an education that would bring the printed page into every Christian household. Here, before the founding of the first American colony, we find the beginnings of adult education, which we fondly regard as our own invention. In the sixteenth century, when the Established Church went in such fear of the sectaries that it made attendance at mid-week prayer meeting a penal offense, sturdy Puritans risked everything in order to teach middle-aged men to read.

These Puritan reformers—Brownists, Independents, Presbyterians, whatever they came to be called later—ultimately set education in New England and Scotland a couple of centuries ahead of education in England. The Stuart kings of the seventeenth century have a great deal to answer for. In one way, we should be grateful to them because their very pigheadedness precipitated the political crises from which came the Bill of Rights. In the history of education, on the other hand, the triumph of a reactionary church hindered what might have been a true democratizing of education. In England today we find two kinds of schools: the so-called public schools like Eton and Harrow, that are so very, very private, and the state-supported schools that carry a stigma of social inferiority. No greater problem of reconstruction faces England at this moment than the problem of rebuilding a school system on something like the American plan. If the Puritans had triumphed in England as they did in Massachusetts, they might have hastened the coming of both public education and social equality.

In the New World in a Puritan society there begins a new chapter in education. Plymouth Colony, to be sure, was founded by lower middle-class people with no particular claim to intellectual eminence, but Massachusetts Bay was a different story. For that we can thank Charles I and Archbishop Laud. What was called the Great Exodus began in 1629 when Charles dismissed his third Parliament. During the following years of autocracy, one of his chief advisers was William Laud, made Bishop of London in 1628 and Archbishop of Canterbury in 1633. Under their regime men of even the most moderate Puritanism began to consider the advantages of living in the New World. These colonists were no ignorant fanatics; they were country gentlemen, men of substance, men with gentlemen's educations or better, doctors, lawyers, scholars. There were clever young men from Cambridge—from Walter Mildmay's Puritan college—who had been what we should call promising undergraduates. There was no promise for Puritans under Charles and Laud, and some of the best minds in England found their way across the Atlantic. It has been estimated that there were proportionately more college graduates in the Colony of Massachusetts Bay than in any country of the Old World.

Boston was settled in 1630. In 1635 the Boston Latin School was founded, for in those days Latin meant education and education meant Latin. In the next year these same men founded Harvard College at Newtown, "dreading to leave an illiterate ministry to the churches when our present ministers shall lie in dust." I do not think you will find it recorded elsewhere in history that an infant colony on a new continent, surrounded by boundless wilderness and beset by all the dangers of famine, disease, and savage neighbors, saw fit in its fifth year to found a Latin School and in its sixth year a college. This was not an accident. It was the inevitable outgrowth of a religious faith that demanded literate congregations and a learned clergy.

This is no place to follow the course of American education step by step. The example was there and the faith was there. In the eighteenth century the force of political doctrine was added. Thomas Jefferson not only wrote the Declaration of Independence but outlined a plan for universal education and founded the University of Virginia. Repeatedly he proclaimed the doctrine that a free people must have an education that was free in every sense of the word. "I have sworn upon the altar of God eternal hostility against every form of tyranny over the mind of man." When he composed his own epitaph he made education the climax of his achievements: "Author of the Declaration of Independence, of the Statute of Virginia for Religious Freedom, and Father of the University of Virginia."

The nineteenth century saw a continuous series of advances in education. The career of Horace Mann and the founding of the first normal schools in 1839 brought new life into the elementary schools. The intellectual ferment of New England transcendentalism inspired such experiments in education as Bronson Alcott's Temple School. Anyone who turns back to Louisa Alcott's *Little Men* or Jacob Abbott's *Rollo at Work* will discover that these are not merely children's books but expressions of a progressive theory of education. Education moved west with the frontier. Colleges like Oberlin and Knox were founded in the same spirit of religious and democratic fervor that had established schools and colleges in the early days of the colonies. The state universities were also conceived and founded in the same faith. From all these came the teachers of the common schools.

Free schools made for democracy, and democracy made for free schools. Nothing is more characteristic of our civilization than the omnipresence of the schoolhouse. I suppose one of the most American things in the world is the schoolmarm. Youngish or oldish, a little prim, a little bossy, a little absurd, she stands squarely at the center of American life.

Of this much we can be sure: Americans believe in schools. We are resolved to have more and better schools in our New Atlantis just as we will have more and better machines, and to our schools we will give an even greater faith. No one who is not actually involved in educational processes can realize the extent of that faith. Come to a great state university like this one in Minnesota and see what boys and girls will do to get an education. Look at the faces of fathers and mothers in a Commencement audience and listen to their voices. Consider that only a small fraction of the fathers who are paying for their children's education have any idea what it is that they are buying. Cynics will say this is only a part of the American passion for getting on in the world. They may explain it as part of the "conspicuous waste" that Veblen ascribed to the leisure class. But anyone who knows students and parents, knows that it is more than this. It is faith.

Faith—"the substance of things hoped for, the evidence of things not seen." What things? Ah, here we come to the question with many answers, the hydra with many heads. What things indeed!

Surely, for one thing, a faith that education will help us to live more competently, get better jobs, make more money, invent more machines, and be constantly richer and happier in the New Atlantis. We hear a good deal of argument about practical or vocational or professional education. In the English-speaking world, education has always been built on a foundation of practicality. I once heard the head of one of the oldest and most aristocratic schools in England insisting that his school was first established as a vocational school. In the Middle Ages it taught Latin because Latin was the *sine qua non* for any kind of clerical job. Harvard College was founded to train ministers. Bacon complained in 1605 that all the colleges of Europe were dedicated to professions, and none "left free to arts and sciences at large." It is a romantic delusion to suppose that education in England and America has ever moved entirely on the intellectual heights. We are a practical people, and we make education work for its living.

The real debate begins whenever a theorist proposes that education shall do nothing *except* serve some immediate practical purpose. A lot of theoretical energy has been devoted to simplifying the school curriculum by dropping out things that were supposedly not useful. It has been asserted that Latin isn't useful, grammar isn't useful, arithmetic isn't useful. The Army and Navy have now discovered that arithmetic *is* useful, at least in wartime, and arithmetic is temporarily reinstated. I remember a P.T.A. meeting at which a school principal explained why arithmetic wasn't taught in his school. He said he remembered the agonies he went through with arithmetic in his childhood, and he wasn't going to make any child suffer that way in *his* school. "Yes," said a friend of mine, "that's all right for the dumb children, but I've got a bright child!"

That brings me to the second point in the American educational creed, the faith that there is some kind of intellectual activity, above and beyond mere useful activity, that belongs to the intelligent mind. I like to think of what the "canine cateress" said to me when I told her that I was afraid my dog wouldn't like her dog food. I said, "He likes to eat what I eat." "Now Miss Jackson," she said, "if you have a good dog, you ought to give him good food!" Pretty generally, we think that the bright child ought to have good intellectual meat. Even the people who don't know exactly what kind of meat that is, believe that the bright child ought to have it. All over the country parents and teachers and clergymen and leading citizens have said, "That's a bright child; he ought to finish high school." "That's a bright child; he ought to go to college." "That's a bright child; we must see to it that he learns how to use his head."

There is another controversial point about education that makes it important to look hard at the American faith and tradition. One section of American opinion nowadays, quite powerful and quite vocal, believes that education should go only so far and stop—just short of any kind of intellectual inquiry into ideas. I won't call names because I don't need to. There are people today who are scared of new ideas about economics and politics just as sixteenth-century conservatives were scared of the dangerous ideas to be found in the Bible. These people want the schools to teach English and science and mathematics but not ideas. They even finance active campaigns to prevent education from getting to the point where it encourages children to ask questions.

If this group of people ever got complete control of the schools, they would produce the kind of education that made Prussianism and Nazism possible. Hitler could never have come into power except in a nation of great intellectual docility. Thirty years ago, before we knew that Germany was dangerous, we used to joke about the importance of the word *verboten*. We said that in America if you put up a sign saying "Don't look," half the town would be crowding around to see what you mustn't look at. In Germany you put up such a *verboten* sign and people go by with their eyes shut.

In all Continental trains there are signs warning you not to lean out of the window. It is dangerous to lean out of the window in French; it is perilous, as I remember it, to lean out in Italian; it is *forbidden* to lean out in German— *Verboten hinauszulehnen!* The sign begging you not to let the children monkey with the fastenings of the compartment doors is in French only. Apparently no German child would ever indulge in such an irregular desire.

As I say, we used to think these things were funny. We don't any more. We have seen the commandments of the Nazi creed:

The Leader is always right.
Whatever serves the interest of the movement, and through it
Germany and the German people, is right.

We have read pronouncements from official university orators defining the Nazi conception of scholarship:

We reject international science. We reject the international republic of learning. We reject research for its own sake. We teach and learn medicine, not to increase the number of known germs, but to keep the German people strong and healthy. We teach and learn history, not to say how things happened, but to instruct the German people from the past. We teach and learn science, not to discover abstract laws, but to sharpen the instrument of the German people in competition with other peoples.

We have learned to fear a scholarship that denies the existence of truth, and an education that seeks not intelligence but uniformity. We have learned to be afraid of a people who always believe what they are told. The Leader says, "Listen. You are the Master Race." Then a docile people says, "*Ja*. Yes, yes, we are the Master Race." The Leader says, "Today you own Germany, tomorrow the world." And a docile people says, "Yes, tomorrow the world." If that is the kind of education that we want in America, the Ethiopian can change his skin and the leopard his spots.

Yet there are people who are moving in that direction and they are powerful enough to be dangerous. Sometimes they attack the teaching of some specific doctrine that seems dangerous to a party in power. That attitude is intelligible but nonetheless dangerous. There are political machines in some southern states, apparently, that would forbid educators and sociologists to teach the facts about the state of Negro schools. I have read attacks on the education of Negroes that might have come straight from *Mein Kampf*. If some news items that I have seen are accurate, teachers have been dismissed for teaching their classes that Hitler's theory of white superiority is false. Any theory which, translated into action, might make trouble for the rulers of the state must not be taught.

In a good many parts of the country (here again I am depending on news items) there have been attempts to specify what facts are to be taught (or not taught) in high school civics courses. There have been attacks on teachers who suggested that some sections of the American population are badly fed. Certain textbooks have been thrown out of the public schools for discussing inequalities in wealth, because such ideas are "un-American." Apparently children must be protected not only from the contamination of social theory but also from any facts that encourage social theorizing. If there is one thing in the wide world that is un-American, this is it. If this sort of restriction is tolerated, if teachers are to be told when they can and cannot tell the truth, then American education will be a totally different article from the one our democracy has put its faith in.

If you don't understand what I mean, look back at the tradition. The sentence from Milton that heads this chapter comes from a defense of the freedom of the press. Only with the free teaching of truth and the free circulation of ideas can you have a free government. "I cannot praise a fugitive and cloistered virtue." "Truth is compared in Scripture to a streaming fountain; if her waters flow not in a perpetual progression, they sicken into a muddy pool of conformity and tradition." "As good almost kill a man as kill a good book."

These are the ideas that Milton's friends brought with them to the New World. It was with faith in the free exercise of reason that American education began. If Milton seems too idealistic, let us turn once more to Bacon, that father of everything that is practical and sane. "Again, for that other conceit that Learning should undermine the reverence of laws and government, it is assuredly a mere depravation and calumny, without all shadow of truth. For to say that a blind custom of obedience should be a surer obligation than duty taught and understood, it is to affirm, that a blind man may tread surer by a guide than a seeing man can by a light."

I venture to say that there is no part of the American tradition more fundamental than this faith in the efficacy of knowledge and education. We believe in education for practical use, education for the training of the active mind, and education for the enlightening of free men in a free state. To be sure, even in the first and easiest of these three we are far short of perfection. Our failure in the third and greatest is enough to make the heart sick. Yet things are known best by their absence. If you think our progress toward perfection is pitifully slight, consider the countries that hold an opposite faith. Look at Germany and Japan, and then turn your eyes back to the English-speaking peoples. Foolish and ignorant we may still be, but at least we have our feet set in a good path and our eyes on the light.

IX

Build Jerusalem

Pray for the peace of Jerusalem:
They shall prosper that love thee.
Peace be within thy walls,
And prosperity within thy palaces.
For my brethren and companions' sakes, I will now say,
Peace be within thee.

PSALMS

Bring me my Bow of burning gold:
Bring me my Arrows of desire:
Bring me my Spear: O clouds unfold!
Bring me my Chariot of fire.

I will not cease from Mental Fight,
Nor shall my Sword sleep in my hand
Till we have built Jerusalem
In England's green and pleasant Land.

WILLIAM BLAKE, Preface to Milton

Beyond the dust and smoke he saw
The sheaves of Freedom's large increase,
The holy fanes of equal law,
The New Jerusalem of peace.

JOHN GREENLEAF WHITTIER, Summer

I saw Immanuel singing   *To be read very softly, but*
On a tree-girdled hill.   *in spirited response.*
The glad remembering branches
Dimly echoed still

116

The grand new song proclaiming
The Lamb that had been slain.
New-built, the Holy City
Gleamed in the murmuring plain.

. . . .

"When this his hour of sorrow   *To be sung.*
For flowers and Arts of men
Has passed in ghostly music,"
I asked my wild heart then—
What will he sing tomorrow,
What wonder, all his own
Alone, set free, rejoicing
With a green hill for his throne?
What will he sing tomorrow
What wonder all his own
Alone, set free, rejoicing,
With a green hill for his throne?

VACHEL LINDSAY, *I Heard Immanuel Singing*

Some city on the breast of Illinois
No wiser and no better at the start
By faith shall rise redeemed, by faith shall rise
Bearing the western glory in her heart.

. . . .

We must have many Lincoln-hearted men.
A city is not builded in a day.
And they must do their work, and come and go,
While countless generations pass away.

VACHEL LINDSAY, *On the Building of Springfield*

Everybody knows the Ancient Mariner, "alone, alone, all, all alone; Alone on a wide, wide sea." Not everybody knows that the author of "The Rime of the Ancient Mar-

117

iner" might have become an American citizen if he had had five hundred pounds. In 1794 Samuel Taylor Coleridge, Robert Southey, and Robert Lovell, the three of them engaged or married to three sisters, contemplated emigrating to America and founding an ideal community on the banks of the Susquehanna. They had talked with an American real-estate agent, who assured them that the district for which he was selling land was admirably suited to such a venture. The climate was ideal. There was no longer any danger from hostile Indians. The soil was so fertile that two or three hours' labor a day would suffice for plentiful crops. Nothing was said specifically about dishwashing and housework, but apparently these also would be marvelously expedited on the banks of the Susquehanna. There were to be long and joyous hours which men and women together could devote to poetry, philosophy, and the flowering of beautiful souls.

The central idea of the colony was simple and logical. In the established societies of the Old World the free exercise of virtue was constantly hampered by heritage and custom, but in America it would be possible to establish new and perfect institutions under which virtue and happiness would flourish hand in hand.

> O'er the ocean swell
> Sublime of Hope, I seek the cottag'd dell
> Where Virtue calm with careless step may stray,
> And dancing to the moonlight roundelay,
> The wizard Passions weave an holy spell.

None were to be admitted into this community but "tried and incorruptible characters." Property was to be held in common, and selfishness was to be nonexistent. These young men felt confident that they would be able "to realize a state of society free from the evils and turmoils that then agitated the world." In fact, they hoped to regenerate the whole state of society, "not by establishing formal laws but by excluding all the little deteriorating passions, injustice, wrath, anger, clamor, and evil speaking, and thereby setting an example of 'Human Perfectibility.' " Their society would be established upon a proper footing. Man would be "considered more valuable than money," and Southey (later a poet laureate) dreamed of tilling the earth in order to "provide by honest industry the meat which my wife would dress with pleasing care."

> And fain would take thee with me, in the Dell
> Of Peace and mild Equality to dwell,
> Where Toil shall call the charmer Health his bride,
> And Laughter tickle Plenty's ribless side!

I have run together quotations from Southey, Coleridge, Lovell, and one of their older and more skeptical friends. Observe the things that are to be combined: virtue, happiness, agricultural and domestic labor (in pleasing amounts), ideal social and political institutions, indifference to money. We have already examined one ideal republic, Bacon's New Atlantis, and seen how many of Bacon's dreams have turned into realities surpassing his expectations. This dream of Coleridge's belongs in quite a different category. Human perfectibility is as far from realization in 1944 as it was a hundred and fifty years ago. It will probably be no nearer to attainment in 2094.

I said also that Bacon's plan for the future was thoroughly American. I shouldn't risk any such rash statement about this project of Coleridge's and Southey's. The typical American dream is certainly not compounded of virtue, agricultural labor, and the absence of money. On the other hand, I believe that it is characteristically American for us to have, here and there in the population, men with exactly this kind of vision. There are more men of this sort in England and America than in almost any other country you could mention. "Your young men shall see visions and your old men shall dream dreams." "Where there is no vision the people perish." "How beautiful upon the mountains are the feet of him that bringeth good tidings."

These visionaries that I am talking about stand out, up and down the centuries, just as conspicuously as the valiant fighters and the lovers of truth. There have been fewer of them, to be sure; they have generally had to stand much ridicule, and often hatred and vilification, but it is part of the history of the English-speaking peoples that such people have lived. Sometimes they have written books like More's *Utopia* and Harrington's *The Commonwealth of Oceana*, explaining how things ought to be. Sometimes they have plunged into the political turmoil of the day, madly believing that the moment has come for the establishing of God's kingdom on earth. Milton and his friends were Englishmen of this type.

> Great men have been among us; hands that penned
> And tongues that uttered wisdom—better none:
> The later Sidney, Marvel, Harrington,
> Young Vane, and others who called Milton friend.

Harrington wrote a book about an ideal republic; the later Sidney, grandnephew of Spenser's friend, wrote discourses on a democratic theory of government more than a hundred years before the American Constitution. Vane, "young in years but in sage counsel old," as Milton wrote, was a Fifth Monarchy man who believed that the Second Coming of Christ was at hand and that Jesus in his own person would bless the new Puritan Commonwealth.

Milton himself played an active and practical part in the struggle between free institutions and an autocratic King, always in the faith that a new dawn was at hand.

Now once again by all concurrence of signs and by the general instinct of holy and devout men . . . God is decreeing to begin some new and great period in his Church. . . . What does he then but reveal Himself to his servants, and as his manner is, first to his English-men? . . . Methinks I see in my

mind a noble and puissant Nation rousing herself like a strong
man after sleep. . . . Methinks I see her as an Eagle mewing
her mighty youth.

Milton, who had dedicated himself to poetry, gave up
eighteen years of his life to controversial prose and the cause
of democracy in England. When the doctors told him that
his eyesight was going fast and that he would lose it entirely if he didn't stop writing, he still went on with his
Second Defence of the English People. In his blindness he
assured his friends that he was supported by his conviction
that the cause was worth the sacrifice. It was enough of a
satisfaction to have lost his eyesight

Overplied
In Liberty's defense, my noble task,
Of which all Europe talks from side to side.

Even after Cromwell's death, when it seemed everywhere
that the cause of the Puritans was lost, Milton was still dic-
tating "A Ready and Easy Way to Establish a Free Commonwealth." He could still believe that God would save
his chosen people—"his English-men" and build a seventeenth-century Jerusalem for his saints.

At the end of the next century another set of visionaries
saw a new and glorious day dawning. This time the sunrise
was in France, but Coleridge and Wordsworth and their
friends felt that the light would shine upon the whole earth.

Bliss was it in that dawn to be alive,
But to be young was very Heaven!

So Wordsworth wrote, looking backward to his young
manhood.

O times,
In which the meagre, stale, forbidding ways
Of custom, law, and statute, took at once
The attraction of a country in romance!

In those days, he said, all gentle and virtuous souls with dreams of a perfect world could work out their ideas

> Not in Utopia,—subterranean fields,—
> Or some secreted island, Heaven knows where!
> But in the very world, which is the world
> Of all of us,—the place where, in the end,
> We find our happiness, or not at all!

Shelley in poem after poem had the same dream of a new and perfect society about to be born. Sometimes he imagined that the inspiration for the ideal world would come from the perfect happiness of a few chosen souls in some place of surpassing loveliness.

> Where for me, and those I love,
> May a windless bower be built,
> Far from passion, pain, and guilt,
> In a dell mid lawny hills,
> Which the wild sea-murmur fills,
> And soft sunshine, and the sound
> Of old forests echoing round,
> And the light and smell divine
> Of all flowers that breathe and shine.

By some blessed effluence the spirit of this happy society would pass mysteriously to the multitudes of men, changing them to its own image of brotherhood.

> And soon
> Every sprite beneath the moon
> Would repent its envy vain,
> And the earth grow young again.

At other times for Shelley the preliminary to the ideal society must be the abolishing of all iniquitous forms of government. That is the vision he saw when he wrote "Prometheus Unbound." In that poem Jove is overthrown, tyranny is destroyed, and veil by veil, evil and error fall away.

                    Soon I looked,
And behold, thrones were kingless, and men walked
One with another even as spirits do.

. . . .

The loathsome mask has fallen, the man remains
Sceptreless, free, uncircumscribed, but man
Equal, unclassed, tribeless, and nationless,
Exempt from awe, worship, degree, the king
Over himself; just, gentle, wise; but man
Passionless—no, yet free from guilt or pain,
Which were, for his will made or suffered them;
Nor yet exempt, though ruling them like slaves,
From chance, and death, and mutability,
The clogs of that which else might oversoar
The loftiest star of unascended heaven,
Pinnacled dim in the intense inane.

In the hearts of all these men, and many others who are
less famous, there lived the common hope of a perfected society on this earth. With this dream of virtue and happiness
went belief in the possibility of physical well-being for all
men, not so much prosperity as a universal sufficiency.
Money-making, covetousness, and theft would all disappear
together, and the free soul would live untrammeled by care
and grow in nobility and strength.

If such were the dreams of the Old World, no wonder
they filled men's minds in America. New England before
the Civil War was full of idealists who were going to build
each his own brand of New Jerusalem. Emerson wrote with
amusement of a convention in Boston in 1840: "Madmen,
madwomen, men with beards, Dunkers, Muggletonians,
Come-outers, Groaners, Agrarians, Seventh-Day Baptists,
Quakers, Abolitionists, Calvinists, Unitarians, and Philoso-
phers." There were people in Boston just as much amused
at Emerson as he was at the Dunkers and Muggletonians.
In fact, it seems to be one of the laws of life that the idealist
gets laughed at. Lowell, at any rate, had the gift of laughing

at himself for "striving Parnassus to climb with a whole bale
of *isms* tied together with rhyme."

> His lyre has some chords that would ring pretty well,
> But he'd rather by half make a drum of the shell,
> And rattle away till he's old as Methusalem,
> At the head of a march to the last new Jerusalem.

Some of the nineteenth-century attempts at ideal living,
solitary or communal, are famous. There was the Oneida
Community in upstate New York that flourished for thirty-
five years. Brook Farm, when Roxbury was still a town and
not part of Greater Boston, was temporarily successful in
a thoroughly uncommercial way and very virtuous and
happy. We have pleasant pictures of Mrs. Ripley, whose
husband organized the colony, rocking the cradle with one
foot while she taught Greek to boys preparing for Harvard.
Hawthorne visited there and reported with exclamation
points that he had milked a cow and that Margaret Fuller's
heifer had hooked all the other heifers. Not far away geo-
graphically Bronson Alcott attempted an ideal existence on
the farm of Fruitlands, drinking only water and living on
"aspiring" vegetables; the baser, down-growing vegetables
like beets were bad for the soul.

Best known, perhaps because of the skill of the teller of
the tale, is Thoreau's practical idyl on the shores of Walden
Pond. William Butler Yeats says that his father read him
Walden when he was a child and that he decided then to
live like Thoreau on the Lake Isle of Innisfree. "Nine bean
rows will I have there, a hive for the honey bee." Those
beans, I suppose, were the Irish descendants of Thoreau's
beans, which he raised and sold, although his Pythagorean
philosophy prevented his eating them! I have read that
Gandhi felt the inspiration of Thoreau, which goes to show
how ideas move round the world.

I have just been reading *Freedom's Ferment* by Alice Felt

Tyler. Her second main section is on cults and utopias, a series of chapters on transcendentalism, millennialism and spiritualism, religious communism in America, and so on. She speaks of more than fifty societies whose inspiration was primarily religious. America had what Europe had not, great tracts of land that could be used as sociological laboratories. Except for the Mormons these people seem generally to have lived in love and charity with their neighbors. If they believed in building Christ's kingdom on earth, it was possible for them to go about it in their several ways without disrupting the economy of their neighbors.

And all that believed were together, and had all things common;

And they sold their possessions and goods, and parted them to all, according as every man had need.

There was room in nineteenth-century America even for the practical communism of the second chapter of The Acts.

Another thing that comes out in Mrs. Tyler's book is the fascination that the New World had for idealists in England and on the Continent. Robert Owen himself, most distinguished of the English socialists of his day, came to try his hand at a utopian colony. Germany, Sweden, and France all sent their contingents. European ideas found a testing ground in purely American societies. Brook Farm in its later years was organized according to Fourier's system of phalanxes, and between forty and fifty other societies were founded on the same plan. "God sifted a whole nation that he might send choice grain over into this wilderness," wrote William Stoughton in 1669; or as Longfellow put it, "God had sifted three kingdoms to find the wheat for this planting." It may seem to us more like natural selection than like the hand of the Lord, but the result is the same. America has drawn to itself from the beginning a disproportionate number of builders of Jerusalem.

But, you may well say, all these dreams ended in failure. A lot of them, like Coleridge's project, never even got started, and the ones that came into being were almost invariably absurd. What is the point in writing a chapter to prove that the English-speaking peoples develop a particularly ridiculous kind of lunacy? Failure I grant. But if you say that these dreams came to nothing, then I could put up a very good case in rebuttal. Of those men who called Milton friend, Harrington was imprisoned and Sidney and Vane were executed. All very well. But some day when you have time, dig into a library of eighteenth-century Americana. Read the sermons and essays and speeches of the men who made the American Revolution. See how they quote Sidney and Harrington and carry their words over into political documents. See how the ideals of the seventeenth-century dreamers came on down into the minds of reformers in the nineteenth century, and see how the vision of one century may become the actuality of the next. Is it not probable that the idealists of the nineteenth century have the same sort of progeny? Is it not probable that all our various experiments for the increased happiness of men in America today are in a way the modern fruit of these ideals?

One of the church fathers said that "the blood of the martyrs is the seed of the church." That is as true of politics as of religion. If you want a faith to flourish, persecute it. Speaking less heroically, don't think that you can destroy a vision by laughing at it—by turning a quart of milk a day into "milk for Hottentots." There may be a martyrdom of laughter, but laughter is good advertising. America is the country of laughter, but also the country where dreams come true.

X   I Do Well to be Angry

And God said to Jonah, Doest thou well
to be angry for the gourd? And he said,
I do well to be angry, even unto death.

JONAH

Avenge, O Lord, thy slaughtered saints, whose bones
   Lie scattered on the Alpine mountains cold;
   Even them who kept thy truth so pure of old
When all our fathers worshipped stocks and stones . . .

JOHN MILTON, *On the Late Massacre in Piedmont*

Avenge the plundered poor, O Lord!
But not with fire, but not with sword;
Not as at Peterloo they died
Beneath the hoofs of coward pride.
Avenge our rags, our chains, our sighs,
The famine in our children's eyes!
But not with sword; no, not with fire
Chastise thou Britain's locustry!
Lord, let them feel thy heavier ire;
Whip them, O Lord, with poverty.
Then, cold in soul as coffined dust,
Their hearts as tearless, dead and dry,
Let them in outraged mercy trust
And find that mercy they deny.

EBENEZER ELLIOTT, *The Jacobin's Prayer*

Who counsels peace, when Vengeance like a flood
Rolls on, no longer now to be repressed;
When innocent blood
From the four corners of the world cries out
For justice upon one accursed head?

ROBERT SOUTHEY, *Ode Written during the
Negotiations with Buonaparte*

O if at length into Age, the last of all stations,
It slides and slows, and its smoky mane of thunder
Thins out, and I detrain; when I stand in that place
On whose piers and wharves, from whose sources and seas,
Men wearily arrive—I pray that still
I may have with me my pities and indignations.

W. R. RODGERS, *Express*

I do not pity the dead, to whom the fierce death came
Like flame, in a wild day or out of a nightmare night. . . .
I pity the mean little minds that remain the same
Despite all that men die for—all men live for, despite!
. . . .
Yes, these I pity—and hate. I light my hate from my pity.
And I pray that it burns to the end of my life, till some
    things I would say are said—
Though it only sand-blast one small stone in one wall of the
    Devil's City.
These are the War Dead I pity. I do not pity the dead.

WILLIAM ROSE BENÉT, *The War Dead*

SOME years ago a life of John Brown was published with
the title *God's Angry Man*. One could write a chapter of
English-speaking history and call it God's Angry Men. For
some reason or other we seem to have a special aptitude for

anger. I don't mean personal anger, because someone has stepped on your foot or stolen your pig. I mean righteous indignation, anger against wrong. I say wrong rather than evil or wickedness because I think that anger at wrong represents this emotion in its purest form. If you are angry at a specific piece of wrongdoing, then your mind is also conscious of the wrongdoer and your feelings may become complicated. There is such a thing, however, as hatred of wrong in itself. In some men it can become a consuming and overmastering passion, destroying sleep and health and overriding all the homely natural human desires. In some men it becomes madness.

I think that as a people we possess a phenomenal capacity for righteous indignation. It isn't one of our universal qualities like courage or friendliness, but it does run through us in very strong streaks. It is much more common, for instance, than the desire to build Jerusalem. In most of us the impulse to prevent or avenge wrong may be passive or latent as we go about our sensible ordinary businesses, but all at once something—some story, outrage, invasion, massacre—touches our imaginations and we flame out with the anger of the Hebrew prophets.

As far as I can make out from history and literature, we are almost unique in this regard. Outside the Old Testament I don't know any literature in which you can find such a persistence of righteous anger as appears in English literature from *Piers Plowman* through *The Grapes of Wrath*. Historically speaking, I don't know where you can find a people so addicted to reformations and righteous revolutions, abolitions of slavery and avengings of Lidice. This doesn't interfere with our being sensible, selfish, and self-seeking in between times—or even at the same time—but it does set us off from the exclusively practical nations who mind their own business and leave everybody else to work out his own damnation by himself.

129

If you want to study the literature of righteous anger, look first at Jonathan Swift. There indeed was a man in whom indignation worked like acid. He wrote the words for his own epitaph: "Where savage indignation can no longer tear his heart." Anyone who thinks of Swift as a man who wrote a nice fairy story for children has completely misunderstood *Gulliver's Travels*. From beginning to end *Gulliver's Travels* is a satire on the animal called man, his vices, follies, and stupidities, his meanness and cruelty and ingratitude, his hypocrisy, and above all his pride. "I hate and detest that animal called man," Swift wrote to Pope. Bolingbroke said of Swift that he was an inverted hypocrite. Most people pretend to be better than they are, but Swift pretended to be worse. "I hate and detest that animal called man, although I heartily love John, Peter, Thomas, and so forth." If John, Peter, and Thomas were in distress there was nothing Swift would not do to save them.

This mixture of indignation and human sympathy appears most startlingly in the Irish pamphlets. Swift was born in Ireland; he lived most of his life in Ireland; he hated Ireland. As a Church of England clergyman he had two Irish parishes at different times, one among Catholics, one among Presbyterians, and it is hard to tell whether he hated the Catholics or the Presbyterians worse. The last thirty years of his life he spent as Dean of St. Patrick's Cathedral in Dublin—and he hated Dublin. All about him he saw poverty and misgovernment. Even Edmund Burke, infinitely calmer minded than Swift, said that the government of Ireland was "as well fitted for the oppression, impoverishment, and degradation of a people, and the debasement in them of human nature itself, as ever proceeded from the perverted ingenuity of man." Swift hated the English for their tyranny and the Irish for their passiveness, hated them both with what the Psalmist called a perfect hatred.

130

The climax came with *A Modest Proposal for Preventing the Children of Poor People from Being a Burthen to their Parents or the country and for Making Them Beneficial to the Public*. In the course of half a dozen years Swift had turned out a series of pamphlets proposing one scheme after another for the improvement of conditions in Ireland. His attack on one particular piece of political graft raised such a furore that even Parliament had to take notice. As Pope said, "The rights a Court attacked, a Poet saved." Then came the final outburst of indignation in the savage irony of *A Modest Proposal*. Modest, moderate, says Swift, really trifling, considering the enormity of the wrong—a proposal to which no one could possibly raise the slightest objection. Here in Ireland, he says, was a population reduced by hunger, filth, and disease to a brutishness lower than that of horses and cattle. Obviously nothing could be done for the adults, who were dying off from starvation and disease as fast as could reasonably be expected. As for the children, how could they be raised to the status not of human beings, to be sure, but at least of well-kept cattle? Clearly by treating them like cattle; by raising them for food!

That is the modest proposal—commercialized cannibalism. Cruel? Not at all. Infinitely kinder than the present method of imposing on them the maximum of human misery.

I desire those politicians, who dislike my overture, and may perhaps be so bold to attempt an answer, that they will first ask the parents of these mortals, whether they would not at this day think it a great happiness to have been sold for food at a year old, in the manner I prescribe, and thereby have avoided such a perpetual scene of misfortunes, as they have since gone through.

In style and manner nothing could be more prosaic, matter-of-fact, and statistical than this essay—number of babies, cost of feeding, probable market—but underneath the dry prose blazes savage indignation in its fiercest form. All you fat landlords, all you smug, self-righteous people who profess and call yourselves Christians, see yourselves for what you are. You courtiers, so convinced of your superiority, so contemptuous of the lower classes! Listen to the *Modest Proposal* and realize that there is no ugliness, no cruelty, no horror, worse than the horror that supports the whole substance of your lives!

It is too much to expect that literature should maintain habitually any such savage fury. It would be intolerable if it did. But all down the centuries comes the echo—I do well to be angry. I heard a lecture last year by J. T. Hillhouse called "The Grapes of Wrath, Some Earlier Vintages." It came in a series dealing with living ideals in national literatures, along with discussions of the parts of our democratic heritage that come from the Old Testament and the classics. The very fact of its appearance in such a list indicates the importance of anger in the English tradition. The speaker included a list of "representative novels containing social criticism," written in England in the eighteenth and nineteenth centuries. Some of them were books of sentiment and pity (I shall return to pity presently), but on the whole it was a list of books of righteous indignation. That is interesting, I think, when you consider that these are novels and that we think of the novel as a type of literature peculiarly designed to give pleasure. You might easily draw the inference that righteous indignation has been an Englishman's idea of pleasure.

There are several points about the list that are worth mentioning. For one thing, this indignant protest against wrong appeared in novels about as soon as there were any novels for it to appear in. If you put the English novelists in chronological order, the first three are Richardson, Fielding, and Smollett, and both Fielding and Smollett stand on this list. Fielding was a lawyer and at one time was justice at the Bow Street police court in London. We know that among other things he drew up a series of proposals for the reform of English criminal procedure. His indignation at the evils of the present system keeps cropping up in the novels even when it has nothing to do with the story. Quite minor characters become involved in miscarriages of justice, not because the structure of the narrative demands it but because Fielding is angry that such things should be. His last novel, *Amelia*, is primarily a description of the misfortunes of people who suffered from the iniquities of the judicial system. He wrote with mingled pity and indignation and with the clear implication that these evils ought to be wiped out.

As you would expect, these novels of indignation piled up in the years following the French Revolution. At the same moment that idealists were looking for the miraculous birth of the New Jerusalem their friends were raging at the evils that somehow or other had failed to disappear. That was the time when Godwin wrote *Caleb Williams*, the year after he had published his monumental work on political justice, which is really a book on the political *in*justice in the world. Somebody asked Pitt, the prime minister, why he didn't suppress *Political Justice*, and he said that he wasn't afraid of a book that cost two guineas (ten dollars and a half)! Novels come cheaper and are easier to read, and *Political Justice* turned into story must have started more waves of righteous anger than Pitt ever dreamed of.

The Adventures of Caleb Williams combines the excitement of a detective story with the moral indignation of a reformer. The murderer Falkland is an aristocrat, actuated by a collection of false notions of honor and protected by a vicious social system that gives him and his class an outrageous and devilish superiority. Falkland first throws the guilt of the crime on two plebeians and then persecutes one of his servants, Caleb Williams, who has discovered the secret, pursuing him with vindictive anger from one misfor-

tune to another. It is only at the end that the essential goodness of Falkland's nature, after a terrific moral conflict,
triumphs over the whole aggregation of evils that make up
society.

As you get into the middle of the nineteenth century the
early Victorian novelists blaze out at the suffering that followed the Industrial Revolution. Here are the miseries of
mine and mill, child labor, slums, all at their worst and
all unmitigated by any kind of humane regulation. Charles
Kingsley, Mrs. Trollope, Charles Reade, George Eliot, and
Mrs. Gaskell are all on my list. We think of Mrs. Gaskell
as the author of *Cranford*, that idyllic picture of the most
charming of English villages—surely a sweet little lady herself, knowing nothing of the facts of life. As a matter of
fact, she was the wife of a clergyman in a big Manchester
parish and had had practical experience as a social worker
among factory hands working for starvation wages. Her
Mary Barton and *North and South* are two of our most
vivid and authentic novels of Victorian indignation.

Greatest of all these writers is Dickens, greatest and most
typically English in the way that anger and sentiment and
absurdity and grotesquerie and goodheartedness are all
churned up together. Slums, poverty, workhouses, debtors'
prisons, Yorkshire schools, the Court of Chancery—no matter which way his anger turned, they were all grist to his
mill. We may think of Dickens with his Pickwicks and
Micawbers, just as we think of Swift in Lilliput and Mrs.
Gaskell in Cranford, but we make a mistake if we leave
out that fire of indignation. He had seen the sufferings of
the poor in his own poverty-stricken childhood. As a small
boy he had seen the inside of the Marshalsea, where his
father was imprisoned for debt. His years as a lawyer's
clerk and then as court reporter gave him a venomous
hatred of courts and lawyers. Not all the things that he
hated were worthy of his indignation, but rage at the

wrongs of the world was for him the very breath of life. Among the novelists he stands as the angriest and most eloquent of all God's angry Englishmen.

I may have been on somewhat disputable ground when I talked about the practical effectiveness of the dreamers, but I have my feet squarely planted on fact when I come to the angry novelists. *Bleak House* led to the reform of the worst evils of the Court of Chancery; *Nicholas Nickleby* practically wiped Yorkshire schools off the map. In America you wouldn't need to go farther than *Uncle Tom's Cabin*. If ever a book set afire the anger that makes history, it is that one. This isn't a history of literature, and I won't follow the tradition down through Frank Norris and Upton Sinclair and Dos Passos and Steinbeck, but the grapes of wrath are stored up in the American heritage and the vintages come early and late.

What about poetry? In the Middle Ages and the Renaissance we have the same story of God's angry man. In the classical tradition anger is one of the emotions that make poetry. We need only look at Milton's sonnets. "Avenge, O Lord, thy slaughtered saints!" So begins the sonnet, "The Late Massacre in Piedmont." It was the atrocity story of the year. A harmless Protestant peasantry had been slaughtered by the soldiers of the Catholic Duke of Savoy, who "rolled mother with infant down the rocks." That wasn't poetic embellishment; that was just a news item. As Cromwell's secretary, Milton drafted the official protest to the Duke of Savoy and letters to Protestant potentates urging them to similar action. And he wrote perhaps his greatest sonnet calling on the Most High God for vengeance.

Milton could also pour forth the vials of his wrath upon iniquity at home.

> For what can war but endless war still breed?
> Till truth and right from violence be freed,
> And public faith cleared from the shameful brand

Of public fraud. In vain doth Valour bleed,
While Avarice and Rapine share the land.

Time would fail me once more if I tried to set down the angry poets who followed the French Revolution. The anger of Coleridge against Pitt, of Wordsworth against entrenched selfishness, of Byron against Wellington and Castlereagh and Metternich and George III, the "old, mad, blind, despised, and dying king" of Shelley's sonnet—these stand in the anthologies for anybody to find.

I met Murder on the way—
He had a mask like Castlereagh.

That is the way poets wrote about bad prime ministers in 1819. Half a dozen years ago I used to amuse myself with scraps of verse in the manner of Shelley.

I saw Murder, saw him plain,
He had a face like Chamberlain,
I saw him when he murdered Spain.

That is bad verse, but a poor twig from a great tree.

Fiercest of all, perhaps, is the anger of Coleridge against Pitt: "Letters four do form his name"; Fire, Famine, and Slaughter are his minions.

Fire. Sisters!—I from Ireland came!
Hedge and corn-fields all on flame,
I triumph'd o'er the setting sun!
And all the while the work was done,
On as I strode with my huge strides,
I flung back my head and I held my sides,
It was so rare a piece of fun
To see the sweltered cattle run
With uncouth gallop through the night,
Scared by the red and noisy light!—
Both. Who bade you do't?
Fire.   The same! the same!
Letters four do form his name.
He let me loose, and cried halloo!

To him alone the praise is due.
All. He let us loose, and cried halloo!
How shall we yield him honour due?
Famine. Wisdom comes with lack of food.
I'll gnaw, I'll gnaw the multitude,
Till the cup of rage o'erbrim:
They shall seize him and his brood.
Slaughter. They shall tear him limb from limb!
Fire. . . . And in an hour would you repay
An eight years' work? Away! away!
I alone am faithful! I
Cling to him everlastingly.

During the last fifty years or so there has been a different kind of poetic atmosphere. We were born into an age of esthetes' poetry, and we are only now struggling out from a kind of poetic hothouse into daylight and fresh air. For the esthete, ideas are anathema. To him an interest in one's fellow man is vulgar and bourgeois. The true poet must be a solitary soul cultivating higher and higher degrees of esthetic sensibility. His only function is to write poetry, and the only function of a poem is to exist. "A poem should not mean but be." Archibald MacLeish has come a long way since he wrote that line, but only a handful of poets have come with him. When Edna Millay wrote "The Murder of Lidice" there were voices lifted on every side to insist that a poet had no right to be angry.

Yet surely Miss Millay and the Benéts and Auden and Spender and their friends have the authority of the centuries behind them.

> In peace there's nothing so becomes a man
> As modest stillness and humility;
> But when the blast of war blows in our ears,
> Then imitate the action of the tiger:
> Stiffen the sinews, summon up the blood!

There is no reason why those lines of Shakespeare's should be extended to include all men except poets. Poets were angry in the last war and they are angry in this, and they do well to be angry.

What then shall we say of the relationship of anger and pity? The question arises naturally as we think of the poetry of 1914 to 1918. It is common today to praise Wilfred Owen as the finest poet of those years. Stephen Spender refers to him in those terms in his preface to *Poems for Spain* and quotes the preface that Owen had sketched out for his own poems. "My subject is War, and the pity of War. The Poetry is in the pity." On the other hand, Yeats refused to give Owen a place in his anthology of modern poetry. Pity was a poor kind of meat for poetry. He was willing to exclude hate, but indignation he must have. "Hate is a kind of 'passive suffering' but indignation is a kind of joy."

It is true that various causes have combined to make pity one of the most characteristic emotions of our age. The same currents of thought that have changed our theories of good and evil have inclined us to the humane emotion of pity and at the same time have made us question our right to be indignant. For Hardy—I am thinking especially of *The Dynasts*—the spirit of pity is the one comforting quality in a sinister and ironic world and the one assurance that mankind can some day emerge from the era of Napoleons and Hitlers. I think it is interesting that in the last war Hardy—at seventy-five—turned from pity to anger.

One of his war poems is a sonnet called "The Pity of It." In the octave he walks in Wessex and listens to the familiar peasant dialect with phrases like "Thu bist," "Er war," "Ich woll," "Er sholl," all so close to the idiom of Germany. Then in the sestet he cries out in rage against the men who bred war between nations so alike in speech and race. "Sinister, ugly, lurid be their fame."

I could turn also to Siegfried Sassoon for poems in which pity turns into anger. There is anger against war, anger against the men who make wars, anger against fat majors, "scarlet Majors at the Base," and generals in the safe places (but in this war generals don't lead such sheltered lives), anger against people at home who sentimentalize over noble soldiers in France but can't be bothered with, the noble soldier home again and out of a job. There is one poem of Sassoon's that says,

Have you forgotten yet? . . .
*Look up, and swear by the green of the Spring that you'll
     never forget!*

Let me end this chapter with a poem of 1943 in which C. Day Lewis takes up the mingling of pity and anger that is the heritage of the English-speaking peoples in time of war.

Will it be so again
That the brave, the gifted are lost from view,
And empty, scheming men
Are left in peace their lunatic age to renew?
Will it be so again?

Must it be always so
That the best are chosen to fall and sleep
Like seeds, and we too slow
In claiming the earth they quicken, and the old
     usurpers reap
What they could not sow?

Will it be so again—
The jungle code and the hypocrite gesture?
A poppy wreath for the slain
And a cut-throat world for the living? that stale
     imposture
Played on us once again?

Will it be as before—
Peace, with no heart or mind to ensue it,
Guttering down to war

Like a libertine to his grave? We should not be
   surprised: we knew it
Happen before.

Shall it be so again?
Call not upon the glorious dead
To be your witnesses then.
The living alone can nail to their promise the ones
   who said
It shall not be so again.

XI   The Ways of
                                   Peace

Her ways are ways of pleasantness,
And all her paths are peace.

PROVERBS

Thus they discoursed together till late at night; and after
they had committed themselves to their Lord for protection,
they betook themselves to rest: the Pilgrim they laid in a
large upper chamber, whose window opened toward the
sun-rising: the name of the chamber was Peace, where he
slept till break of day, and then he awoke and sang . . .

JOHN BUNYAN, *The Pilgrim's Progress*

Peace hath her victories
No less renowned than war; new foes arise.

JOHN MILTON, *To the Lord General Cromwell*

As long as our civilization is essentially one of property, of
fences, of exclusiveness, it will be mocked by delusions. Our
riches will leave us sick; there will be bitterness in our
laughter, and our wine will burn our mouth. Only that
good profits which we can taste with all doors open and
which serves all men.

RALPH WALDO EMERSON, *Napoleon*

There is an American spirit. There are American ideals. We
are members of one body, though it is a varied body. It is
inconceivable that we should follow the evil path of Europe

and place our reliance upon triumphant force. . . . We
shall continue to present to our sister continent of Europe
the underlying ideas of America as a better way of solving
difficulties. We shall point to the *Pax Americana*, and seek
the path of peace on earth to men of good will.

FREDERICK JACKSON TURNER, *The Significance of Sections
in American History*

Only the gracious heart returned,
. the summer-blossoming soul and the kindled stars;
children unafraid in meadows, laughter
billowing from the unsinister skies;
God, only these. . . .

EMMANUEL LITVINOFF, *Not Revenge . . . But These*

"God, give us peace! not such as lulls to sleep,
But sword on thigh, and brow with purpose knit!
And let our Ship of State to harbor sweep,
Her ports all up, her battle-lanterns lit,
And her leashed thunders gathering for their leap!"

JAMES RUSSELL LOWELL, *The Washers of the
Shroud*, OCTOBER 1861

In war, resolution; in defeat, defiance; in victory, mag-
nanimity; in peace, good-will.

WINSTON CHURCHILL, QUOTED BY SIR EDWARD MARSH
IN *A Number of People*

Writing in the midst of a world at war, I find my mind
dwelling on random reminiscences of peace. Many of them
come back to me with a new and more insistent meaning.
I think, for instance, of a college lecture that I heard at

Radcliffe in the fall of 1914. The lecturer, an authority on the state of Europe, adjusted his eyeglasses, smiled urbanely at his audience, and began, "Probably none of you has ever seen a soldier." I don't doubt that he used that line a great many times in the course of the winter, talking in other colleges and to churches and women's clubs. If by a soldier you meant, as he did, an enlisted man in the United States Army, you could have made that statement safely almost anywhere in the United States except within range of the military posts. We talked it over in the dormitory that night and had to admit it: None of us had ever seen a soldier.

That sentence has recurred to my mind many times in many places. In France, for instance. All my memories of France belong to the years between the wars. Except when I was in Paris, I have never been in France without being beset by the feeling that this was a country in which no one could live without thinking of soldiers. So many times I have stood watching freight trains at grade crossings, every single car bearing its legend that told how many men it could carry to the front. Eight horses, forty men; eight horses, forty men; eight horses, forty men. There's going to be another war.

Like so many Americans, I have always been in love with France. I cherish my memories of good food, good wine, and good weather, and all the friendly, busy people in a peaceful land. I like to recall the exchange of greetings, the appreciations of weather and scenery, the *merci's* and *adieu's* that attended each most insignificant transaction such as the purchase of a cake of soap. My heart warms at the memory of the brisk little shopkeepers who sold me Tauchnitz editions and Edgar Wallace in French with an effusiveness worthy of first folios.

At the same time, I remember the soldiers—youngsters in badly fitting blue-grey uniforms leaning out of third-class coach windows; Algerians at Arles, very trim in blue and red uniforms with fezzes; Senegalese at Fréjus. And always the freight trains. Eight horses, forty men. There's going to be another war.

Another friendly, peaceful country that comes to my mind is Norway. I was there only once, in the summer of 1934. War was less than six years away, but there was nothing that spoke to the tourist of wars past or wars to come. I remember all sorts of casual conversations on trains and at hotels. I think of a man harnessing horses to take a party of tourists to the next fiord. He was glad to know that I was from Minnesota; he was from South Dakota himself, he said, but he thought Minnesota was a good state.

Most vividly there comes back to me the picture of a handful of tourists in a Norwegian railroad carriage. There were two Italians, mother and daughter, an Englishman, myself, and a Japanese professor of agriculture being conducted from Oslo to Bergen by a Norwegian professor of agriculture. The conversation was largely in English, supplemented by French and German, and was full of information about farming in Norway, with special attention to cereal crops. We all craned our necks to see the *saeters*, the summer farms apparently inaccessible, high up the mountainside. I remember too the stops at mountain railroad stations where big cheerful people with knapsacks got on and off, and Edgar Wallace in Norwegian was for sale in the station bookstalls. I remember saying to myself again and again, "This is a country I must come back to."

My mind turns next to an island half the world away where I found myself a year later. The juxtaposition of five nationalities in a Norwegian railway coach seemed a mere nothing compared with my students and fellow teachers at the University of Hawaii. I contemplated my classbook with a never-ending delight. I never quite got accustomed to teaching the history of English literature (from Beowulf to Matthew Arnold) to Chang, Chang, Ching, Ching, Chow, Choy, Chun, and Chun. The O's in that course were exclusively Japanese: Ogawa, Ogi, Okada, Okamoto, Okano, Okazaki, Osumi. I liked the combination of ancestries in the W's and Y's: Watrous, Whittington, Wilson, A. L. Wong, Charlotte Wong, Felice Wong, K. L. Wong, Minnie Wong, K. Yamanoto, M. Yamanoto, and Basil, Bernard, Bernice, and Elizabeth Young.

I still think of the Japanese janitor who took care of my office. Our first and practically our only conversation was on the subject of mosquitoes. He trotted off and came back with something that made a vile brown smoke and caused far less discomfort to the mosquitoes than to me. After that I found a single hibiscus in a vase on my desk each morning. The blossoms were of all sizes and colors, plain and ruffled, single and double, some of them of the most extraordinary delicacy, so that I would find myself studying the veining instead of getting on with my themes. The little janitor did our building early and disappeared for the day, and it was weeks before I got a chance to thank him. He was happy I liked them. He liked them. He grew them, seventy kinds. All this came out with many smiles and jerks and practically no verbs. He liked me and he liked hibiscus; that was all I ever knew about him.

I put last, though chronologically they belong earlier, a Christmas Eve and Christmas Day in London in 1933. I was staying at a Bloomsbury boarding house, a place frequented by American graduate students and college professors because it was close to the British Museum and had something which purported to be central heating. The proprietor was a naturalized German-Jew; the manageress was an Irish Catholic from Dublin. There was a jolly Scotch-Irishman from Belfast. There were two Scotch ladies, Covenanter stock, very precise and delightful. There were two absurd old gentlemen who gave the impression of having materialized out of Dickens. There was an elderly and impoverished widow, whose husband had belonged to the same family as the hero of *The Faerie Queene*, Book V.

At a table in the corner was a German woman with her two youngsters home from a Quaker school in Kent, and three German friends that they had brought from school for the holidays. They had German Christmas cookies, a Christmas tree all their own, and a circle of candles. They were among the first of Hitler's exiles, and they were celebrating their Christmas Eve in London because they were Jews.

I remember half a dozen Americans the next morning, listening to King George V. It was two winters before he died. He was broadcasting to the whole Empire, and he expressed his rejoicing that improved facilities in communication were being used increasingly for the mutual understanding of all parts of the British Commonwealth. "We owe something of the change to modern science; but her gifts would have been useless without the sanity, the patience, and the good will of all my Peoples. For it is on such qualities that the foundations of national, as of personal, life are laid—unshakable sanity, invincible patience, and tireless good will."

All these memories taken together, I think, carry with them a good handful of implications about the ways of a world at peace. Of all the people I have mentioned, not one was hoping for war, with the possible exception of the Japanese professor that I met in Norway, and I have no real right to except even him. I am willing to believe he may have been studying European agriculture in order to help Japan raise more food *without* going to war. As for the rest, they were all typical, cheerful, peaceful people, making friends with strangers and wishing them well. In France there were reminders that peace was temporary; in

England one looked nervously at the German exiles and wondered what their presence foreboded. In Norway and Hawaii one felt as though peace might last forever.

As I think back over all these people, it seems to me that they have a kind of common quality or combination of qualities, which is the hallmark of the peace-loving peoples. I find it very hard to define. It has nothing to do with race; it seems independent of money or social position; it has no immediate connection with religion, though I think that its roots are Christian. As King George said that Christmas Day, it implies sanity, patience, and good will. It implies enjoyment of life and the capacity for both busyness and leisure. It carries with it a certain self-sufficiency and independence. It includes a kind of miscellaneous curiosity, about hibiscus in Hawaii or *saeters* in Norway, ranging from agriculture to Edgar Wallace. If I have learned anything in my odds and ends of travel, I have learned that peace is something more than the absence of war. It is something positive that creates a kind of civilization of its own.

It would be pleasant to think that this was peculiarly true of America. With all our faith in peace, in liberty, and in the pursuit of happiness, should we not have developed special qualities of mind and heart? I wonder if strangers look at us and say, "These are such splendid people, they must have grown up in a good society! Here are people who know how to live."

There are shelvesful of English and American books that seem to prove that I am talking nonsense. I think, for instance, of the latest novel of H. G. Wells, *You Can't Be Too Careful,* which professedly devotes itself to showing that the modern English-American-European world is so constituted that it produces human beings of the most despicable type. I may have misunderstood Wells, but I have always felt in his work a kind of contempt for the human race, even in the early fantasies like *The First Men in the Moon* and *The Country of the Blind*. I have much the same feeling when I read the novels of John Dos Passos. If I understand what he has to say, war may bring out the worst in human nature, but peace maintains a kind of uniform miscellany of meannesses and stupidities. His characters seem to have no interests except money, sex, and communism, and they get no pleasure out of any of these three. I must have read dozens of books like that since 1920.

"All great nations learned their truth of word, and strength of thought, in war," wrote Ruskin in *The Crown of Wild Olive*. "They were nourished in war, and wasted by peace; taught by war, and deceived by peace; trained by war, and betrayed by peace;—in a word, they were born in war and expired in peace." William James once wrote an essay which he called *The Moral Equivalent of War*, and the core of his argument was that peace atrophies certain qualities that we can ill afford to do without. Early in this war I learned a rhyme by Louis MacNeice.

> In the Nineteen-Twenties
> Life was gay;
> They made the clock run
> Until it ran away.
>
> Ten years later
> In a desert place
> They met the clock again
> With murder in his face.

Is this what comes of peace and the pursuit of happiness?

It is possible that we have been a little too smug in our peacefulness, a little too inclined to take literally Franklin's aphorism that there never was a good war or a bad peace. After all, what do we do with peace when we have it? We make money, we spend money. We make ourselves comfortable. We kill time. We turn on the radio. We get out the car and go somewhere. We keep one eye on the Joneses.

These things in themselves are neither good nor bad. On the other hand, even in a good peace, bad things may fatten, like white slugs under a stone. Making money may be necessary, desirable, and pleasant, but the pursuit of money to the exclusion of everything else seems to be very bad for the soul. When Milton parceled out the sins among the several fallen angels, he made Mammon "the least erected spirit that fell from Heaven."

> For even in Heaven his looks and thoughts
> Were always downward bent, admiring more
> The riches of Heaven's pavement, trodden gold,
> Than aught divine or holy else enjoyed
> In vision beatific.

That has been one of the commonest charges against American civilization, that we have let the love of money blot out all things divine and holy, and commonplace things like honesty and kindliness as well. In the last two years we have had evidence that for some men it has destroyed patriotism. If peace becomes identical and coextensive with the pursuit of profits, surely there is something wrong with peace.

I notice that most of the patriotic anthologies of these last years have sections devoted to descriptions of American life. In one book this section is called "The Pursuit of Happiness." We have a habit of using the phrase out of its context and making it an end in itself, and used in this way it suggests another of the charges that critics have brought against peacetime America. They say that we are determined to run after pleasure though the sky falls. We all have acquaintances today who seem resolved to go through this war on that principle. War or no war, they will resist any interference with their pursuit of happiness.

149

However the war is to be won, it will have to be managed without inconveniencing them.

I feel convinced—and this is the main idea of this chapter—that the great test of peace or democracy or any other institution is the kind of people it develops. We can hardly deny that our years of peace have produced some pretty selfish and unscrupulous people, and even some rather reprehensible national traits. Moreover, these qualities seem to be due, in part at least, to our habit of putting our trust in peace and prosperity. If as a nation we are mad about money and mad about pleasure, we may well wonder if our faith in our system of society is well bestowed or justifiable.

If, I say. But personally, I cannot accept the premise. I have the schoolteacher's habit of observing people and wondering if they are doing right. I like to see people doing right, and I find that observing the people round about me is much more comforting than reading reports from Congress. It gives me much greater assurance that the right sort of people have been growing up in America at peace. Let me start with the neighborhood I live in.

It is a very ordinary neighborhood and, from the standpoint of the novelist, very dull. There is nobody within miles who could be described as wealthy. There are a few good-sized houses, built when children and servants were plentiful, but railroad tracks and grain elevators have closed in on us, and the big houses are being cut up into apartments. There are quite a few university people here, faculty, students, and janitors. Most of the others have small businesses or fairly good jobs. In the bad years there were some families on relief. Most of us take care of our own houses, gardens, and cars, and do our own shopping. We talk to each other without being introduced. I know the first names of the children and dogs and the surnames of practically no one. Although it is part of a largish city, it is much the sort of community that William Allen White used to write about in Emporia, Kansas.

Now it is my observation that most of these neighbors of mine, regardless of income, lead interesting and intelligent lives—rather pleasant, civilized lives such as I was describing at the beginning of the chapter. They seem fond of their families. They are nice to each other. I have never stalled my engine or been stuck in a drift but what someone has come along and given me a push. I believe that friendliness is as much a mark of a good civilization as cruelty is of a bad one. I have always felt that "laughter, learnt of friends; and gentleness" is the most important line in Rupert Brooke's sonnet, "The Soldier." It is one evidence of a good civilization if a soldier remembering home remembers laughter learned of friends, and gentleness, and "hearts at peace under an English heaven."

I notice that these people do a great many simple, innocent things that are part of the American tradition. Almost to a man they work on their lawns and gardens. "God Almighty first planted a garden," wrote Bacon. "And indeed it is the purest of human pleasures. It is the greatest refreshment to the spirits of man." He said also that there is nothing "more pleasant to the eye than green grass kept finely shorn." (I wonder if the pleasures that are best for the soul are not the ones that do not have to be pursued too violently!)

My neighbors and I like to rest our eyes on green grass and exchange bits of advice about cutworms. The annual progress of a mole from one end of the block to the other starts uncounted conversations. Sunday afternoons in early spring are rich in great decisions about the moving of peonies and the best disposal of iris. I am not ascribing any miraculous efficacy to nature. I merely think that in actual experience the growing of gardens makes men more humane and gracious. It is a specific against envy, hatred, malice, and all uncharitableness—barring envy of one's neighbors' tulips and uncharitableness toward one's neighbors' dogs. One of Raymond Clapper's last dispatches described an army hospital in New Guinea where the doctors have all sorts of techniques for rehabilitating their patients, "but it is gardening that seems most of all to heal the soul."

There are plenty of occupations besides gardening that cultivate sanity, patience, and good will in a peaceful world. Playing games seems to be a good thing. In the 1930's chairmen of cricket clubs used to write serious letters to the London *Times* explaining that if Hitler had been a cricketer he wouldn't have had all these wrong ideas. Absurd as the letters sounded even then, there was truth in them. The kind of mind that can get contentment out of cricket—or baseball or golf—belongs to a more healthy civilization than the mind that finds its sport in torturing Jews.

I think that we should put fishing down among the avocations that are good for the soul. I have never tried to introduce *The Compleat Angler* to my neighbors, but I am sure that many of them would find Walton a sympathetic character. They would understand how his friend Sir Henry Wotton felt about fishing. " 'Twas an employment for his idle time, which was then not idly spent, a rest to his mind, a cheerer of his spirits, a diverter of sadness, a calmer of unquiet thoughts, a moderator of passions, a procurer of contentedness." He said also "that it begat habits of peace and patience in those that professed and practiced it."

I am inclined to think that a studious preoccupation with machines and engines is another source of patience and civility. I like to remember two high school boys who acquired an incredibly ancient car and pushed it home to their back yard. Every Saturday morning they took the engine apart. Piece by piece they fingered it, wiped it, oiled it, blew on it, prayed over it, and then with agonized concentration they put the whole thing together again. They cranked the engine, they listened reverently, they diagnosed its every rattle. Sometimes they even drove around the block. Then the dismemberment would be repeated. They weren't exceptional boys in any way but they were very earnest and gentle and good as they worked over that engine. There must be a great many boys like that tinkering with the engines of jeeps and planes and tanks today.

No one of these things in itself will save the soul of a man or a nation. Or, for that matter, not all of them together, with a good many books and art institutes and symphony concerts thrown in. But taken as a whole, they make up the soil and the atmosphere in which good souls grow. Almost any pursuit that demands care, attention, and precision, and particularly something that involves a certain amount of independent judgment—like what kind of bait to use in casting for certain kinds of fish, or what tools to use in repairing a household gadget—seems to enhance the excellence of life. It is a kind of prophylactic against egotism and paranoia. Almost literally it restoreth the soul. As I think of my neighborhood multiplied over the continent, I can't help believing that people of good hearts and good will outnumber the money-grabbers by many times.

Yet in many places this kind of simple, comfortable living is as remote as the New Jerusalem. There are towns where no plant will grow and rivers where no fish swims. There are whole communities where the capacity for civilized enjoyment has been almost destroyed by poverty. There are cities of which Richard Aldington's "Whitechapel" is the symbol.

> Noise;
> Iron hoofs, iron wheels, iron din
> Of drays and trams and feet passing;

Iron
Beaten to a vast mad cacophony.

In vain the shrill far cry
Of swallows sweeping by;
In vain the silence and green
Of meadows Apriline;
In vain the clear white rain—

Soot; mud;
A nation maddened with labour;
Interminable collision of energies—
Iron beating upon iron;
Smoke whirling upwards,
Speechless, impotent.

In vain the shrill far cry
Of kittiwakes that fly
Where the sea waves leap green.
The meadows Apriline—

Noise, iron, smoke;
Iron, iron, iron.

Can the ways of peace be pleasant when they are laid
on soot and mud, surrounded by iron and noise, clouded
by smoke? I don't know, but I have the unalterable conviction that they can be made much more pleasant than
they are. In Charles A. Beard's new book, *The Republic*,
I was particularly interested in the chapter on "the general
welfare" and all the interpretations and limitations that
have attached to that phrase. Speaking still as a schoolteacher, I think that phrase, general welfare, means the
general welfare in infinite extension. It includes the wiping
out of conditions that make the good life impossible and
the cultivating of institutions under which good souls can
grow. The older American tradition never boggled too
much over jurisdiction and constitutionality when there
were good things that needed to be done. Finding the machinery for building better lives for more people is one of
the problems of American peace.

Another of the great problems of peace is the mingling and harmonizing of all the peoples of diverse civilizations who have come to make their homes in this country. It is a slow and difficult process. It must be true that neighborliness and gardens and fishing and tinkering have played their part. In some communities amalgamation moves rapidly. In others generations of association seem only to intensify ingrown prejudices. It was the hope of the nineteenth-century poets that the new American character would be a synthesis of all the virtues of all our component peoples.

> Sparta's stoutness, Bethlehem's heart,
> Asia's rancor, Athens' art,
> Slowsure Britain's secular might,
> And the German's inward sight.

So wrote Emerson in the years when Germany stood for philosophy and wisdom!

It was the hope of Longfellow as well. When he gathered his tellers of tales in the Wayside Inn, it was with deliberate intent that he put the Norwegian, the young Sicilian, and the Spanish Jew side by side with the New Englanders. He thought that out of such interchanges of culture America would grow to maturity.

As the blood of all nations is mingling with our own, so will their thoughts and feelings finally mingle in our literature. We shall draw from the Germans, tenderness; from the Spaniards, passion; from the French, vivacity,—to mingle more and more with our English solid sense.

In these days when prejudices have been intensified by war, it does no harm to remind ourselves that a hundred years ago the virtues ascribed to Germany were insight and tenderness and that numberless Germans came to this country out of love of liberty and hatred of militarism. The first German I ever knew was an elderly gentleman who had come to Massachusetts in his romantic youth to fight in the Union Army and help liberate the slaves. The school-master in Louisa Alcott's *Little Men* is her father idealized, and she made the portrait even more idealistic by making him a German.

This is not a year when one can ask a large audience to listen to the virtues of the Japanese. The stories that come from the Pacific are too horrible, too outrageous. Yet I cannot forget the Japanese janitor who brought me hibiscus, or one Japanese freshman who learned more than all the other students in the class put together and seemed possessed by an almost intolerable earnestness to learn everything there was to be known. Of all the Japanese that I met in ten months in Hawaii, only one showed me anything but unfailing friendliness and courtesy. I don't think this was hypocrisy. I think the Japanese who live on the Islands believe in friendliness as part of American civilization. They eat American food and grow six inches to a foot taller than their rice-fed grandparents. They wear American clothes and play American football. They have Young Men's Buddhist Associations that do the same things as the YMCA, and they sing "Buddha loves me, this I know" to the American Sunday School tune. The Japanese students that I taught at the University of Hawaii were making themselves American in as many ways as they knew how, and they could have given lessons in courtesy, if in nothing else, to some of the native-born Americans who were paying thirty dollars a day at the Royal Hawaiian Hotel.

When the war is over we shall go back to the slow ways by which peace makes one civilization out of the fragments of many. I remember that after the last war there was a little burst of enthusiasm for what was called Americanization. Universities gave courses in Americanization, in which, as I understood it, students learned how to go out and Americanize immigrants. I am not sure that our efforts were directed toward the right people. It seems to me that the groups that need the most missionary work are the ones who regard themselves as already perfect (and uniquely perfect) in their Americanism. Nothing is more completely at odds with the American tradition than the bigotry and prejudice of certain third-to-tenth-generation Americans. Regrettably enough, a self-righteous mental stagnation seems to be among the perennial products of peace.

Karl Shapiro has a poem called "University" that begins this way:

> To hurt the Negro and avoid the Jew
> Is the curriculum.

It ends with a contrast between the snobbishness and prejudice of the university and the dream of Jefferson when he founded it.

And the true nobleman, once a democrat,
Sleeps on his private mountain. He was one
Whose thought was shapely and whose dream was broad. . . .

"Behold, how good and how pleasant it is for brethren to dwell together in unity," said the Psalmist. In these days the spacious dream of brotherhood that Jefferson dreamed seems even farther away than we had realized. The war has brought to the surface all sorts of hatreds and animosities—against Jews, Negroes, Japanese, Mexicans, "foreigners"—but the potential hatreds must have been working in men's souls through all these years. These emotions also have been among the works of peace! Sanity, patience, and good will, to quote once more from King George's Christmas message, are apparently not things that grow of themselves. "Peace hath her victories," as Milton said, but she has also her heartbreaking failures. I wish I knew where to turn to find the leaders and teachers who will bring our feet back into the ways of fellowship. One can teach children, immigrants, the poor; one can teach anyone whose heart is eager to learn. But how can one teach grown men of power and substance, who are convinced that the American gospel is a gospel of hate and whose wrongness is armored with righteousness?

One other question comes into my mind. What happens to patriotism in the long years of peace? Does it flourish and grow strong, or does it languish almost to the point of death and require an occasional war to revive it?

As far as literature goes, I think that patriotism has a way of dropping out of the picture between wars. I have heard literary critics declare that it is an obsolete emotion and no longer acceptable in literature. Only our more jingoistic and imperialistic statesmen talk about it much, and the more they talk, the more the serious-minded people worry. Frankly, I have rarely heard a so-called patriotic speech in peacetime that didn't fill me with a profound distrust of the speaker's intelligence, honesty, and good taste. It is not characteristic of Americans at peace to rhapsodize over love of country.

We may well have developed a distrust for the kind of unreasoning devotion to fatherland that has been cultivated by Germany and Japan. As I recall my high school German, I think that some of the poetry must have been chosen with the idea of instilling a reverence for German patriotism in our unwary minds.

> Truest love until the grave,
> To thee I swear with heart and hand;
> For what I am and what I have
> Thank I thee, my fatherland.

That is my hasty translation of one piece of high school German as nearly as I can remember it. Whatever our ideas may be, they don't sound like that. I suppose it is American to think that the people make the fatherland, not the fatherland the people.

I don't know what degree of self-conscious patriotism is good for us in times of peace, but I can think of one kind that has been growing up among us. I have in mind an affection for the actual physical land, such as filled the novels of Thomas Wolfe. It certainly goes well back into the last century. One of the poems of Longfellow that has lasted best is the poem on Portland—"Often I think of the beautiful town That is seated by the sea."

> I can see the shadowy lines of its trees,
>   And catch, in sudden gleams,
> The sheen of the far-surrounding seas,
> And islands that were the Hesperides
>   Of all my boyish dreams—
>
> I remember the black wharves and the slips,
>   And the sea-tides tossing free;
> And Spanish sailors with bearded lips,
> And the beauty and mystery of the ships,
>   And the magic of the sea.

It is hard to be affectionate toward all America at once. There is such a thing as a typical English landscape— hawthorn hedges, cows knee-deep in grass, swans on the river, skylarks in the sky. The American who goes to Stratford-on-Avon takes a deep breath and says, "This is England! This is what I came to see." There is no typical American landscape. Loving Portland and Casco Bay will never teach you to love flat prairies. Yet American literature has grown increasingly rich in poetry that expresses this kind of patriotism. That is the spirit in which Stephen Vincent Benét wrote "American Names."

> I have fallen in love with American names,
> The sharp gaunt names that never get fat,
> The snakeskin-titles of mining-claims,
> The plumed war-bonnet of Medicine Hat,
> Tucson and Deadwood and Lost Mule Flat.

. . . .

I will remember Carquinez Straits,
Little French Lick and Lundy's Lane,
The Yankee ships and the Yankee dates
And the bullet-towns of Calamity Jane.
I will remember Skunktown Plain.

I will fall in love with a Salem tree
And a rawhide quirt from Santa Cruz,
I will get me a bottle of Boston sea
And a blue-gum nigger to sing me blues.
I am tired of loving a foreign muse.

. . . .

I shall not rest quiet in Montparnasse.
I shall not lie easy at Winchelsea.
You may bury my body in Sussex grass,
You may bury my tongue at Champmédy.
I shall not be there. I shall rise and pass.
Bury my heart at Wounded Knee.

It is also the spirit of Malcolm Cowley's "The Long Voyage."

Not that the pines were darker there,
nor mid-May dogwood brighter there,
nor swifts more swift in summer air;
    it was my own country,

having its thunderclap of spring,
its long midsummer ripening,
its corn frost-stiff at harvesting,
    almost like any country,

yet being mine; its face, its speech,
its hills bent low within my reach,
its river birch and upland beech
    were mine of my own country.

Now the dark waters at the bow
fold back like earth against the plow;
foam brightens like the dogwood now
    at home, in my own country.

XII   *Faith and Fire*

Who through faith subdued kingdoms, wrought righteousness, obtained promises, stopped the mouths of lions,
Quenched the power of fire, escaped the edge of the
sword, from weakness were made strong, waxed mighty
in war, turned to flight armies of aliens.

HEBREWS

If to feel, in the ink of the slough,
And the sink of the mire,
Veins of glory and fire
Run through and transpierce and transpire,
And a secret purpose of glory in every part,
And the answering glory of battle fill my heart;
To thrill with the joy of girded men
To go on forever and fail and go on again,
To be mauled to the earth and arise,
And contend for the shade of a word and a thing
      not seen with the eyes:
With the half of a broken hope for a pillow at night
That somehow the right is the right
And the smooth shall bloom from the rough:
Lord, if that were enough?

ROBERT LOUIS STEVENSON, If This Were Faith

I say that the real and permanent grandeur of
      these States must be their religion,
Otherwise there is no real and permanent grandeur;
(Nor character nor life worthy the name without religion,
Nor land nor man or woman without religion.)

WALT WHITMAN, Starting from Paumanok

An American Credo

Where was he going, this man against the sky?
You know not, nor do I.
But this we know, if we know anything:
That we may laugh and fight and sing
And of our transience here make offering
To an orient word that will not be erased. . . .

EDWIN ARLINGTON ROBINSON, *The Man against the Sky*

Faiths blow on the winds
and become shibboleths
and deep growths
with men ready to die
for a living word on the tongue,
for a light alive in the bones,
for dreams fluttering in the wrists.

CARL SANDBURG, *The People, Yes*

Then let us from the patient land
Take strength, nor fail to share the charmed
Routine of stars, or trysting keep
With common things, with evenings warmed
By music, food, and love, and sleep.

For present solace these, but for
Our hope we've nowhere else to look
Except into our spirit's book.
No hell unspilled by lords of war
Upon the people's flesh has ever
Parched the human heart's endeavour,
The human will to love and truth.
For one face mired in black unruth
A score will signal us each day
The sun unquenched within our clay.

Across the tundra of our dread
We must beat on, windbitten, to
The unseen cabin's light, and through
The glooming western firwoods thread,
In hope to pass the peaks terrific
And win the wide sundrenched Pacific.

EARLE BIRNEY, *On Going to the Wars*

What of the faith and fire within us
　　Men who march away
　　Ere the barn-cocks say
　　Night is growing gray,
To hazards whence no tears can win us;
What of the faith and fire within us
　　Men who march away?

THOMAS HARDY, *Song of the Soldiers*

WHAT of the faith and fire within us? Hardy asked
that question in 1914. I hear gloomy voices answering:
There is no faith, no fire; only a flash in the pan. The great
ages of faith are past. There were centuries, long ago,
these voices tell us, when everyone believed and everyone
was happy. In those days there were great poets like Dante,
great thinkers like St. Thomas Aquinas. Then the great
cathedrals "rose like an exhalation" all over Europe. It
seemed to Emerson that they rose out of the heart of
Christianity.

The hand that rounded Peter's dome
And groined the aisles of Christian Rome
Wrought in a sad sincerity,
Himself from God he could not free.

163

In those blessed days all men worked and worshipped together. How pitiful we seem in contrast; how uncertain, how contradictory, how distraught!

I hear cheerful voices too. Faith? Outworn superstition. Thank God we've got rid of that old stuff. Science has taught us better. And I hear a third set of voices, also cheerful and a little condescending. Dear me, they say, we don't bother about creeds any more, do we? Don't we all believe in the same things underneath? What does it matter anyway?

Starting with the last group first, I rise to contradict them. I insist that what we believe matters very much. I think the words of Epictetus are still true after nearly nineteen hundred years. "Neither death, nor exile, nor pain, nor anything of this kind is the real cause of our doing or not doing any action, but our inward opinions and principles." The ideas men believe in make all the difference in the world in the lives they lead. The ideas that dominate a community determine whether or not that community is good to live in. It is the ideas of a country that make that country worth fighting for.

How about the idea that science has put an end to faith? The answer to that is simple and unequivocal. Science and faith deal with different bodies of fact. The subject matter of science is the physical and material universe. Science will produce exactly the same information about that physical universe, regardless of whether it is or is not the work of God. The scientist as an individual may have religious (or irreligious) convictions. The priest as an individual may have accurate or inaccurate scientific conceptions. If the two men come into conflict, it is when one of them is trying to set up jurisdiction in the other's territory.

What, then, about the lament that the ages of faith are past? There are authors who glorify the twelfth century and the thirteenth, before Protestantism stirred in Wycliffe and Huss, or science in Copernicus and Bacon. I have friends who feel like Robinson's Miniver Cheevy, "born too late." If only they had lived in the days of the Crusades, how religious and happy and devoted they would have been! Yet how much, after all, do we really know about those great ages of faith? Of all those devout Christians, only a handful could read and write. Certainly the great masses of the people never left any record of the state of their souls. The parish priests might have told us, but they were no book writers. It is true that the Crusades got fought and the great cathedrals got built. Some writers would have us believe that every time a workman lifted a cathedral stone, he said, "I am doing this happily for the glory of God." Personally, I doubt it; I very much doubt it. I imagine that men working in the great ages of faith thought about the things that men working still think about in this world today. I doubt if they stayed overtime laying one more stone for the glory of God. I think they straightened their backs and cursed their rheumatism and wondered if there was anything good for supper. I would lay any amount of money that there were workmen at Salisbury and Chartres who had no more religious emotion than their modern counterparts in Detroit and Chicago.

It is true enough that America is full of religious confusion and contradiction. How could it be otherwise in a nation with our ancestry? We need only look back at our origins—Congregationalists and Baptists in New England, "the dissidence of dissent and the protestantism of the Protestant religion"; William Penn's Quakers in Pennsylvania; Lord Baltimore's Catholics in Maryland; Scotch-Irish Presbyterians in the middle colonies; Dutch Protestants in New York; Swedish Protestants in Delaware; French Huguenots in South Carolina; Anglicans up and down the coast. Consider how many varieties of religion have come to our continent since the Revolution, and how many peculiar and particular revelations have been made to seers and prophets on our own soil. Deploring the absence of One True Church in America is as sensible as lamenting that we don't possess the Philosopher's Stone or the Fountain of Youth.

But a study of this same history might lead us to another conclusion and a very interesting one. American history can show us an almost unparalleled record of belief in the *importance* of faith. The New World was peopled by men who would rather fight for their existence as Congregationalists, Catholics, or Quakers than live in comparative security as ostensible members of a church they could not believe in. I am not ignoring the fact that there were always colonists who came for completely unreligious motives—to get rich, perhaps, or to keep out of jail. Even making the utmost allowance for motives of this sort, Americans still show a phenomenally high percentage of ancestors who came to this country for what they conceived to be the truth. If we still bear the marks of our miscellaneous religious origins, it is reasonable to suppose that we keep also something of our ancestors' faith in faith.

We can look in vain in America for any *Quicunque vult:* "Whosoever will be saved, before all things it is necessary that he hold"—the Catholic faith or any other "which except a man believe faithfully, he cannot be saved." When the Episcopal Church of the United States dropped the Athanasian Creed out of its Book of Common Prayer it did a characteristically American thing. It is much more American to say with Emerson, "The faith that stands on authority is not faith," or with Whittier, "Better heresy of doctrine than heresy of heart." You could even say that the American spirit spoke in Dante when he wrote that sometimes to doubt the justice of God was not heresy but highest faith. Today Wordsworth, Shelley, Emerson, and

Browning are all quoted constantly by Christian teachers
and preachers, yet none of the four accepted the teachings of the churches into which they were born. In one
sense of the word they were "faithless," yet at the same
time they were passionately believing. They believed with
an intensity that nothing could shake, and their faith still
rings through their verse.

Could we, I wonder, make up a kind of American creed
that most of us could subscribe to, leaving to each man
the right to add any other theological paragraph that his
conscience demanded? Perhaps not. Perhaps, though, we
could make a kind of rough draft of an American creed
by asking, What would you like to be able to believe in?
Let me try that for a few pages.

What would we like to believe in? Should we start by
trying to find some phrase for God, something like Matthew Arnold's "the not-ourselves that makes for righteousness?" I imagine that that would come nearer the end than
the beginning. The beginning would be with men. I want
to believe in men, or Man, in human nature, in the goodness of human nature, the goodness of men and the potential goodness of men. I want to believe in a reality of
goodness in other people and in myself. And I want other
people to believe in the same thing.

If someone said to me, "That is what I want to believe
in," I should say, You can, as long as you limit yourself
to believing this—that men have the capacity for goodness
and that that capacity is often realized. You can't believe
that all men are always good unless you have a preter-
natural power to be blind to facts. But for evidence of
goodness, it is all about you. You can start with the historical records, "Verdict which accumulates From length-
ening scroll of human fates." However you make up your
list of virtues—goodness, kindness, courage, justice, courtesy, honesty, loyalty, service to one's fellow men, or

what you will—you will find them as part of recorded fact. In civilizations where courage has been esteemed a great virtue, the records are full of brave men. If another age exalts religious faith, men will be found who burn at the stake for the truth of God as they see it. In even the most purely factual account of any era in history you will find records of good men.

Beside the record of history stands the testimony of poets and storytellers. Poetry, taking it by and large, is a record of beliefs, just as history is a record of facts. When Shakespeare said that Brutus stabbed Caesar he was writing what he believed to be fact. When he built up the character of Brutus—single-minded, idealistic, loyal to the ideals of republican Rome and yet gentle with an Elizabethan courtesy—he was making a kind of profession of faith. "I, William Shakespeare, believe in men like this." In some of the earlier chapters I have multiplied instances of this kind of poet's testimony. I could add the lines that Matthew Arnold wrote in Emerson's *Essays*.

> Yet the will is free;
> Strong is the soul, and wise, and beautiful;
> The seeds of godlike power are in us still;
> Gods are we, bards, saints, heroes, if we will!—

If you want a third kind of confirmation, do what the poets did, poets like Chaucer, Shakespeare, Spenser, Wordsworth, Longfellow. Look about you. What you see will depend partly on what sort of person you are. As Bacon said, all our judgments are deluded by the idols of the cave, and we see what our personal make-up predisposes us to see.

A few years ago I read a volume of essays called *Living Philosophies*. The editor had written to a long list of distinguished men—scientists, economists, men of letters, and so forth—asking them for their personal philosophies of life. There were quite a number who said that they didn't believe in the existence of God or of the human soul. They frequently ascribed this skepticism to science, but in actuality they seemed to be basing it on personal experience. Theodore Dreiser, as I remember it, said that he didn't believe in souls because he had never been able to detect any signs of a soul in himself or in anyone else he knew. That isn't a question of science; that is just a matter of temperament or psychological make-up. I presume there have always been people like that. Our present scientific attitude makes it easier for men to tell the truth about themselves, which I take to be a good thing both for them and for us.

H. L. Mencken, in the same group of essays, said that he couldn't conceive what is meant by the Holy Ghost. That is not the presence of science but the absence of imagination. The idea is simple enough. A great many men have felt the spirit of God within them and written down what they felt. Very frequently in reading their books you can understand what these writers are talking about, even if you have never had the experiences yourself. But if you can't, you can't. In that case, as I said before, it is probably better to say so. I imagine that it is a good thing all around for men with spiritual incapacities to admit them frankly, like color blindness or tone deafness.

You may be so constituted that your mind dwells upon manifestations of evil. Even so, you may still be able to find goodness if you set yourself to look for it. It is well to remember the principle of logic about the difficulty of proving a negative. You don't disprove the existence of bravery by showing that there are cowards living at the same time with the heroes, or even that there are more cowards than brave men. We have no comparative statistics for this age or any other. The point is that no number of instances of cowardice can destroy the fact of courage;

no amount of brutality can destroy the fact of kindness; no amount of time-serving and hypocrisy can contradict the fact that up and down the centuries men have been willing to give their lives for truth. You remember how Abraham argued with the Lord, "Peradventure there are fifty righteous within the city." As the Lord challenged him, he went on down—forty-five righteous, forty, thirty, twenty. "Peradventure ten shall be found there." If there are ten righteous, then there is righteousness, and it is possible to start a creed with faith in the goodness of men.

What else do we as Americans demand of our creed? Second, I think, a belief that life is worth while, apart from its intrinsic pleasure and in spite of its intrinsic pain. We want to be something more significant than a biological mechanism, "a thing of watery salt, held in cohesion by unresting cells." We want to see some sort of meaning in all this business of living, working, thinking, loving, and having children. We should like to think of ourselves as essential components of some larger order, human or divine, by whose nature our conduct is justified. In one of Dorothy Sayers's books she sees a group of university women, heterogeneous, chattering, slightly ridiculous, as "fused into a corporate unity with one another and with every man and woman to whom integrity of mind meant more than material gain—defenders in the central keep of Man-soul, their personal differences forgotten in face of a common foe." It would be a satisfaction to most of us to feel ourselves fused into such a corporate unity of mankind.

Is this faith in the worth-whileness of life a possible faith? Again, I should say yes, perfectly possible. At the very least, its validity can never be disproved. At its best, it gives one a fellowship with the saints of God. And on a middle ground, where most of us live, it affords the kind of assurance that will carry us through the Sloughs of Despond. There may be no proof by recourse to history, but there is nonetheless a mounting total of evidence of experience. When a doctrine is not susceptible of logical proof, it is sensible to ask if it works, and works for people of our sort. If large numbers of intelligent men in the English-speaking world have lived in the faith that life is worth while and have worked hard to the end of their days on that assumption, that in itself is a kind of evidence. People who believe that life is good find it good. "Better to wear out than rust out," said a seventeenth-century bishop.

> For still the Lord is Lord of might;
> In deeds, in deeds, he takes delight;
> The plough, the spear, the laden barks,
> The field, the founded city, marks;
> He marks the smiler of the streets,
> The singer upon garden seats;
> He sees the climber in the rocks;
> To him, the shepherd folds his flocks.
> For those he loves that underprop
> With daily virtues Heaven's top,
> And bear the falling sky with ease,
> Unfrowning caryatides.
> Those he approves that ply the trade,
> That rock the child, that wed the maid,
> That with weak virtues, weaker hands,
> Sow gladness on the peopled lands,
> And still with laughter, song and shout,
> Spin the great wheel of earth about.

That quotation comes from Stevenson. I have another quotation, a single sentence from a twenty-year-old note-book, "It was good in those days to have courage and faith, an axe, and trees." I don't know where I got it; maybe from a book, maybe from a lecture, but I think most probably from a freshman theme. I think it was written by a boy remembering what his grandfather told him about the Minnesota frontier. It is a good American sentence in any tense—past, present, or future. It stands as a symbolic instance of one great article of our American creed.

What for a third point? This, I think: We want to believe that in the long run goodness and justice and right will triumph. However evil the temporary appearance or the apparent outcome, we wish to believe that under the aspect of eternity, reason and the will of God will prevail. When Hardy answered his own question, "What of the faith and fire within us?" that was his answer—"In our heart of hearts believing Victory crowns the just."

That was an astonishing answer from a man who for most of his life had seen man as the victim of "purblind Doomsters," but it is one more testimony in a long tradition. We have to thank Winston Churchill for reminding us of Clough's "Say Not the Struggle Nought Availeth."

> Say not the struggle nought availeth,
> The labor and the wounds are vain,
> The enemy faints not, nor faileth,
> And as things have been they remain.
>
> If hopes were dupes, fears may be liars;
> It may be, in yon smoke concealed,
> Your comrades chase e'en now the fliers,
> And, but for you, possess the field.
>
> For while the tired waves, vainly breaking,
> Seem here no painful inch to gain,
> Far back, through creeks and inlets making,
> Comes silent, flooding in, the main.
>
> And not by eastern windows only,
> When daylight comes, comes in the light,
> In front, the sun climbs slow, how slowly,
> But westward, look, the land is bright.

I could pile up quotations from America. First Lowell:

Truth forever on the scaffold, Wrong forever on the throne,—
Yet that scaffold sways the future, and, behind the dim unknown,

Standeth God within the shadow, keeping watch above his
    own.

Then Whittier:

> I turn me, awe-struck, from the sight,
>   Among the clamoring thousands mute,
> I only know that God is right,
> And that the children of the light
>   Shall tread the darkness underfoot.

And finally, Emerson:

> Stainless soldier on the walls,
> Knowing this,—and knows no more,—
> Whoever fights, whoever falls,
> Justice conquers evermore,
> Justice after as before,—
> And he who battles on her side,
> God, though he were ten times slain,
> Crowns him victor glorified,
> Victor over death and pain.

Faith is not proof, and faith may be wrong, but this
particular faith carries over into a transcendental world a
great many related American habits of mind. The traditions of the New Atlantis and the New Jerusalem here join
hands; the scientists, the preachers and prophets, the teachers, and God's angry men all live in this same conviction.
It is American to believe that right will triumph and very
American to gird up our loins against the foe and see to it
that right *does* triumph.

A faith in the possible goodness of men, a faith in the
goodness of the individual life as part of a good whole,
a faith in the ultimate triumph of justice and right—even
in an age of many faiths and many heresies, these three
beliefs stand out. No Athanasian creed, to be sure, but a
pretty firm foundation for a country's life.

"For here lay the excellent wisdom of him that builded
Man-soul," wrote Bunyan in *The Holy War*, "that the

walls could never be broken down, nor hurt, by the most mighty adverse potentate, unless the towns-men gave consent thereto."

> This England never did, nor never shall,
> Lie at the proud foot of a conqueror
> But when it first did help to wound itself.

This Man-soul, this England, this America. The souls of men and the souls of nations live by the same laws. By birth and by inheritance we have the qualities and the faiths of a free and good people. It is not by any adversary from without that our citadel can be shaken.

Acknowledgments

Grateful acknowledgment is made to the following publishers for permission to use poems or excerpts from poems and prose published, and in most instances copyrighted, by them.

JONATHAN CAPE LIMITED. For the poem "Will It Be So Again?" by Cecil Day Lewis, from the volume *Word Over All;* first published in the *New Statesman and Nation,* May 1, 1943.

THOMAS Y. CROWELL. For stanzas from "The Magpies in Picardy," by T. P. Cameron Wilson, from *War Verse* (1918), edited by Frank Foxcroft.

DODD, MEAD & COMPANY. For the stanza from "The Dead," by Rupert Brooke, from his *Collected Poems* (1915).

DOUBLEDAY, DORAN & COMPANY. Holders of the American copyright, for excerpts from the poems of Rudyard Kipling (*Rudyard Kipling's Verse: Definitive Edition,* 1940); used with the permission also of Mrs. George Bambridge, daughter of the late Rudyard Kipling.

E. P. DUTTON & COMPANY. For lines from the poem "Aftermath," by Siegfried Sassoon, from the volume *Picture-Show.*

FARRAR & RINEHART. For passages from "American Names" and "John Brown's Body," by Stephen Vincent Benét, from *The Selected Works of Stephen Vincent Benét.*

FAVIL PRESS (LONDON). For lines from the poem "Not Revenge . . . But These," by Emmanuel Litvinoff, from the volume *Conscript.*

L. B. FISCHER. For the passage from the novel *Mud on the Stars,* by William Bradford Huie.

HARCOURT, BRACE & COMPANY. For lines from "Express," by W. R. Rodgers, from *Awake! and Other Wartime Poems* (1942); and for passages from *The People, Yes* (1936), by Carl Sandburg.

HARPER & BROTHERS. For lines from the poem "Silence in Mallorca," by Genevieve Taggard, from her *Collected*

176

Acknowledgments

PRINCETON UNIVERSITY PRESS. For an excerpt from *The Meaning of the Humanities* (1938), by Ralph Barton Perry; and for lines from the poem "The Battle of Maldon," from *Old English Poetry* (1922), by J. Duncan Spaeth.

G. P. PUTNAM'S SONS. For the excerpt from "Dunkirk," by Winston Churchill, from the book *Blood, Sweat, and Tears.*

RANDOM HOUSE. For lines from the poem, "I Think Continually," by Stephen Spender, from his *Poems* (1934).

REYNAL & HITCHCOCK. For lines from the poem "University," by Karl Shapiro, from his volume *Person, Place and Thing* (1942).

THE RYERSON PRESS. For the poem "On Going to the Wars," by Earle Birney, from *David and Other Poems* (1942).

MARTIN SECKER & WARBURG, LTD. For lines from "Oak and Olive," by James Elroy Flecker, from his *Collected Poems.*

Acknowledgment is made also to the following periodicals, for permission to use the material listed.

Minnesota Chats (University of Minnesota)—For paragraphs from a talk broadcast by Dean John T. Tate (October 1942).

The New Republic. For lines from "In Memory of W. B. Yeats, II," by W. H. Auden, issue of March 8, 1939; for the poem "The Clock," by Louis MacNeice, issue of June 3, 1940; for the poem "No Man Knows War," by Edwin Rolfe, issue of July 19, 1939; and for the excerpt from "Silence in Mallorca," by Genevieve Taggard, issue of August 20, 1938, since appearing in a volume published by Harper & Brothers. Acknowledgment is made also to the authors.

The New Statesman and Nation. For excerpts from the speech on German Empire Day, by Kahrstedt, quoted in the issue of April 24, 1937, and from an editorial about Leslie Howard in the issue of June 12, 1943.

The New York Times. For the poem "Captain Colin P. Kelly, Jr.," by Robert Nathan, published in the magazine section, December 21, 1941. Acknowledgment is made also to the author.

The Observer, London. For lines from "Personal Valour," by Victoria Sackville-West.

Poetry. For the poem "Galileo Goes to War," by Preston

Newman, in the issue of January 1944. Acknowledgment is made also to the author.

The Proprietors of *Punch*. For the poem "There Is No Sanctuary for Brave Men," by A. G. Herbertson, in the issue of October 30, 1940.

The Saturday Review of Literature. For lines from the poem "The War Dead," by William Rose Benét, in the issue of January 29, 1944; acknowledgment is made also to the author and to Alfred A. Knopf, who will publish the poem in the volume *Day of Deliverance*. Also for "Of England," by Stuart Cloete, issue of October 5, 1940.

Acknowledgment is made also to the following authors, who gave personal permission to quote from their work. Except in instances in which details of the material used are given below, they appear elsewhere under Acknowledgments.

Richard Aldington, for the poem "Whitechapel," from his *Collected Poems* (London: Allen & Unwin); William Rose Benét; Hewlett Johnson, Dean of Canterbury, for one of his pilgrim's prayers; Nicholas Moore, for a stanza from "The Ruin and the Sun," from the volume *The Glass Tower* (London: Nicholas & Watson, 1944); Robert Nathan; Preston Newman; Edwin Rolfe; Genevieve Taggard; Laurence Whistler.

INDEX OF QUOTATIONS